LESS & SERENE

TABLE OF CONTENT

1. FOUNDATIONS OF MINIMALISM
2. MINIMALIST LIVING ROOM
3. DINING SPACES
4. SERENE BEDROOMS
5. MINIMALIST KITCHENS
6. MINIMALIST ENTRIES & HALLWAYS
7. LUXURIOUS MINIMALIST BATHROOM
8. THE MINIMALIST HOME OFFICE
9. MINIMALISM OUTDOORS
10. GALLERY OF INSPIRATION

11	ESSENCE OF JAPANDI
12	NATURAL MATERIALS AND TEXTURES
13	JAPANDI FURNITURE ESSENTIALS
14	JAPANDI LIVING SPACES
15	SERENE BEDROOMS & BATHROOMS
16	THE JAPANDI KITCHEN & DINING
17	WABI-SABI: BEAUTY IN IMPERFECTION
18	JAPANDI AND NATURE
19	SUSTAINABLE JAPANDI

Less & Serene
by StudioLux

©2025 StudioLux. All Rights Reserved.

No portion of this book may be reproduced, distributed, or transmitted through any means—including photocopying, recording, electronic, or mechanical methods—without prior written authorization from StudioLux, except for brief excerpts included in critical reviews or specific noncommercial contexts permitted by copyright regulations.

The contents presented in this book serve solely educational and inspirational objectives. StudioLux has endeavored to ensure accuracy and comprehensiveness; nevertheless, it does not offer warranties or assurances regarding the exactness or applicability of the provided information, nor will it assume responsibility for any potential errors, omissions, or inaccuracies. Readers are advised to apply their own judgment and discretion when adopting the concepts or techniques featured in this publication. StudioLux accepts no liability for losses or damages incurred directly or indirectly through the utilization or dependence on information provided herein.

All trademarks, registered trademarks, product names, company names, and logos referenced within this work belong exclusively to their respective owners.

First Edition
Cover and Layout Design by StudioLux

BECOME ICONIC—MAKE YOUR STYLE VIRAL WITH US

You've selected "Less & Serene", a statement addition to your beautiful home.

Now it's your moment in the spotlight! Create a captivating video or sophisticated photograph featuring "Less & Serene" and share your creation on Instagram, TikTok, or Facebook using the hashtag #StudioLux. Your elegant post might just spark the next big social media trend!

Why participate?

- Showcase your exquisite taste and inspire a wide audience.
- Gain the opportunity to be featured by StudioLux for greater visibility and recognition.

And there's more to come...

CLAIM YOUR EXCLUSIVE GIFTS!

To celebrate your creativity, we've designed an exclusive bonus filled with practical and inspiring ideas you can immediately use to enhance your home's style. Don't miss this special opportunity—it's your next step toward achieving interior excellence.

Follow these simple steps to claim your reward:

1. Capture your unique photo or create a compelling video featuring the book.
2. Share your creation on Instagram, TikTok, or Facebook using the hashtag #StudioLux.
3. Scan the QR code below to instantly unlock your exclusive bonus content.

Your moment of viral fame awaits!
With style and appreciation,

StudioLux

MINIMALIST

SL

STUDIOLUX

INTRODUCTION

Discovering Minimalist Luxury

Luxury is often misunderstood, frequently associated with extravagance, excess, and opulence. Yet, true luxury is subtle, defined by thoughtful simplicity and precision—qualities perfectly embodied by minimalism. Minimalist luxury isn't about deprivation; rather, it's about clarity, intentionality, and quality. It speaks to a lifestyle that values mindfulness, sophistication, and timeless elegance.

In the bustling, visually crowded landscape of contemporary living, minimalist luxury emerges as a quiet revolution. It invites you to appreciate the richness inherent in restraint, guiding you towards spaces that inspire serenity and encourage purposeful living. Imagine entering a room where every element—furniture, artwork, textiles, lighting—has a reason for being there. Nothing is superfluous; nothing is accidental.

This mindful curation not only elevates aesthetics but transforms the way you interact with your surroundings. A minimalist luxury interior isn't merely seen; it's felt. Each carefully selected piece whispers of quality craftsmanship, thoughtful design, and refined taste. Materials—natural wood grain, smooth marble, textured linens—are allowed space to breathe, radiating their intrinsic beauty without competition.

Minimalist luxury also champions the essence of well-being. Spaces stripped of unnecessary distractions create mental clarity, reducing stress and promoting an elevated state of living. Every detail is meticulously considered, turning homes into sanctuaries that nurture rather than overwhelm.

Through this journey into minimalist luxury, you'll discover how the interplay of space, light, materials, and careful selection can yield a sense of profound satisfaction. It's not about living with less; it's about surrounding yourself with what truly matters, curating environments that enhance the quality of your life.

In this book, you'll learn to master this art form, transforming spaces from mere environments into expressions of intentional elegance. Welcome to minimalist luxury—the pinnacle of contemporary design philosophy, where less is unquestionably more.

Why Less Truly Means More

At first glance, the concept of minimalism might appear restrictive—perhaps even austere. Yet, beneath the surface lies a philosophy that offers unparalleled freedom and depth, emphasizing quality over quantity, presence over abundance. It is an intentional practice that transforms spaces into genuine reflections of the individuals who inhabit them.

Minimalism's true power lies in what it allows you to experience rather than possess. By thoughtfully curating your living environment, you remove visual and emotional noise, creating clarity not only in your space but also in your mind. With fewer distractions, your focus shifts naturally toward the quality, function, and harmony of each chosen element, enhancing your connection with everything you surround yourself with.

Consider this: when a space is cluttered, each item competes for your attention. In contrast, minimalist interiors thoughtfully highlight the beauty and craftsmanship of select pieces. Rather than drowning in excess, these pieces are elevated, making their quality, form, and texture infinitely more impactful. A meticulously crafted wooden chair or a beautifully textured linen sofa becomes more than furniture—it becomes art, meaningful through both its visual simplicity and its meticulous construction.

Furthermore, minimalist spaces provide practical, psychological, and emotional benefits. Research consistently demonstrates that uncluttered environments reduce stress and anxiety, increase productivity, and improve mood. By embracing less, you're not only curating a refined aesthetic but also nurturing your mental and emotional health.

Yet minimalism does not mean sacrificing comfort or warmth. Instead, it prioritizes genuine comfort, achieved through thoughtful design, exceptional quality, and understated luxury. Every object serves a deliberate purpose, contributing to a cohesive narrative that tells the story of thoughtful living. This intentional approach ensures that each piece you choose truly resonates with you, fostering deeper appreciation and satisfaction.

Ultimately, minimalism teaches us that true luxury isn't found in excess or abundance but in simplicity and refinement. When thoughtfully applied, this principle creates spaces filled with meaning, clarity, and emotional depth—environments that genuinely enrich daily life.

In embracing minimalism, you'll discover that less genuinely means more: more beauty, more peace, and more fulfillment. Welcome to the profound art of living simply yet beautifully.

CHAPTER 1
FOUNDATIONS OF MINIMALISM

Core Principles of Minimalist Interior Design

At its essence, minimalist interior design is not just an aesthetic—it's a philosophy centered on purposeful living. Mastering minimalism demands understanding the foundational principles guiding every design decision, ensuring that every choice reflects intent, clarity, and elegance.

Here are the core principles that define minimalist interior design:

1. Intentional Simplicity

Minimalism prioritizes purposeful simplicity. Every object and element in your space must have clear value or function. Items included solely for aesthetics still serve the intentional purpose of beauty and balance. This disciplined approach prevents clutter, fostering spaces that are calming and purposeful.

2. Functional Form

Minimalist design emphasizes form following function. Furniture and decor should not only look good—they must primarily be practical. A minimalist home prioritizes ergonomic efficiency, comfort, and usability, where each item is thoughtfully chosen to enhance lifestyle rather than merely occupy space.

3. Visual Harmony and Balance

Balance is crucial for creating serene, minimalist interiors. Each element should complement the others, creating visual harmony without overwhelming the eye. Achieving balance involves careful consideration of scale, proportion, and symmetry, guiding the selection and arrangement of furniture, lighting, and accessories.

4. Uncluttered Spaces

Minimalist interiors cherish open spaces as vital design elements. Negative space (the empty areas around objects) isn't wasted—it intentionally enhances your appreciation of selected furnishings. This openness creates breathing room, allowing occupants to focus fully on the quality and detail of their surroundings.

5. Quality Over Quantity

Minimalism champions quality over sheer quantity. Investing in fewer, higher-quality items results in durable, timeless interiors. Furniture and decorative elements should be thoughtfully selected, crafted from materials designed to withstand the test of time both aesthetically and functionally.

6. Restrained Color Palette

Color selection in minimalism is intentional and restrained. Neutral tones—white, beige, greys, and muted earth tones—create a soothing foundation. Limited use of color ensures coherence, allowing textures, materials, and forms to take center stage without visual distractions.

7. Natural Light and Openness

Ample natural light is essential in minimalist interiors, illuminating spaces naturally and warmly. This openness creates an inviting and expansive feeling, vital to enhancing minimalist aesthetics. Window treatments remain minimal, focusing on transparency or sheer elegance to maximize daylight.

8. Detailed Craftsmanship

In minimalism, every detail matters. Precision, quality craftsmanship, and meticulous attention to detail distinguish minimalist spaces. Whether a meticulously designed light fixture, carefully chosen hardware, or bespoke furniture, each element speaks of intentional craftsmanship and thoughtful selection.

9. Continuity and Flow

Minimalist interiors are characterized by seamless transitions and coherent flow between spaces. Flooring, color schemes, and materials unify different rooms, creating an overarching sense of harmony. This continuity enhances the spaciousness and tranquility inherent in minimalist living.

Natural Palettes: Mastering Neutral Colors

Color profoundly impacts how we perceive space, influencing not only aesthetics but also mood, clarity, and well-being. In minimalist interiors, neutral palettes are not just a design preference—they are essential tools used to create a harmonious and serene environment. Mastering neutral colors means understanding their subtleties, qualities, and powerful potential to shape a minimalist space into a refined sanctuary.

Understanding Neutral Colors

Neutrals are sophisticated tones that are muted, subtle, and versatile. Common neutral shades include whites, creams, grays, taupes, beiges, and soft earth tones. Their understated elegance effortlessly enhances interiors, offering quiet luxury without overwhelming the senses.

- White: Timeless, clean, and expansive, white visually enlarges spaces, creating openness and purity.
- Cream and Beige: Warm neutrals, providing a cozy yet refined ambiance.
- Gray: From subtle dove gray to deep charcoal, it brings depth, sophistication, and versatility.
- Taupe and Earth Tones: Offering grounded elegance, these neutrals naturally connect interior spaces to their surroundings.

Selecting and Combining Neutral Colors

Minimalism thrives on restraint and intention, making careful selection and thoughtful combination of neutrals essential. When choosing a palette, focus on subtle gradations and harmonious transitions.

Monochromatic Schemes:
- Utilize variations of a single neutral shade, creating subtle depth through layering textures and tones. For instance, pairing soft ivory walls with creamy furniture, textured linen upholstery, and plush rugs creates sophisticated layers of visual interest.

Complementary Neutrals:
- Mixing complementary neutrals, such as cool grays with warm beige or ivory with subtle earth tones, introduces nuanced contrasts. These balanced interactions enhance depth and maintain visual harmony.

Accent Neutrals:
- Incorporate deeper neutrals such as charcoal, chocolate brown, or slate as accent colors to anchor the space, lending contrast without compromising minimalism's inherent tranquility.

Using Neutral Colors Effectively

Neutral palettes shine brightest when thoughtfully implemented across various interior elements:

Walls and Ceilings:
- Prefer lighter neutrals to amplify light reflection, enhance spaciousness, and foster calmness.

Flooring:
- Opt for neutral flooring materials, such as natural wood, polished concrete, or stone. These materials not only complement minimalist aesthetics but also add texture and warmth.

Furniture:
- Choose upholstery and furnishings in nuanced neutral shades to create coherence and sophistication.

Decorative Textiles:
- Introduce visual interest through natural fabrics—linens, cottons, wool—in varying textures, all within your chosen neutral palette.

Artwork and Decor:
- Select minimalistic art and decorative objects that blend subtly yet purposefully, echoing the neutral scheme.

Lighting and Neutral Palettes

Lighting significantly impacts how neutrals are perceived. Natural daylight best enhances neutral colors, creating an airy, fresh ambiance. Artificial lighting—especially soft, warm LED lighting—should reinforce the palette without distorting its integrity.

Benefits of Neutral Palettes in Minimalism

Neutrals offer compelling practical and psychological advantages:

Calmness and Clarity:
- Neutrals reduce visual noise, promoting relaxation, mindfulness, and mental clarity.

Timelessness and Versatility:
- Neutral palettes remain timeless, easily adaptable to changing tastes, styles, and trends without necessitating major redesigns.

Highlighting Quality:
- Subtle colors emphasize craftsmanship, materials, and design quality, allowing the inherent beauty of textures and forms to take center stage.

Mastering neutral palettes in minimalist design requires thoughtful restraint, nuanced selection, and strategic application. Done correctly, neutral colors become the backdrop of refined living, quietly luxurious and enduringly elegant, transforming homes into serene, welcoming sanctuaries.

Essential Materials: The Power of Wood, Stone, Glass, and Textiles

In minimalist interior design, material selection is an art form in itself. The chosen materials carry immense responsibility—they provide the essential character and depth to minimalist spaces, balancing visual purity with tactile sophistication. Wood, stone, glass, and textiles are not merely aesthetic choices; they embody minimalism's core principle of authenticity, transforming interiors into spaces defined by understated luxury and sensory richness.

Wood: Warmth and Authenticity

Wood brings organic warmth, timeless elegance, and a grounding quality that makes it an indispensable material in minimalist interiors. Whether rich walnut, smooth oak, or pale birch, wood's natural grain and texture subtly enrich minimalist spaces, providing visual warmth without clutter.

Choosing the Right Wood:
- Opt for sustainably sourced hardwoods like oak, walnut, or ash for durability, beauty, and ethical considerations. Lighter woods like pine or birch offer brightness and airiness, while darker woods introduce depth and contrast.

Application in Interiors:
- Wood is ideal for flooring, cabinetry, furniture, and accent walls. The craftsmanship should be impeccable, celebrating the natural textures without excessive adornment.

Stone: Timeless and Enduring

Stone embodies permanence, strength, and sophisticated restraint. From marble's subtle veining to limestone's earthy textures, stone introduces authenticity, durability, and calm elegance to minimalist interiors.

Stone Selection:
- Marble, granite, limestone, and slate each offer unique textures and colors. Marble conveys refined luxury, limestone provides subtle earthiness, granite ensures robustness, and slate offers sleek modernity.

Interior Applications:
- Use stone for flooring, countertops, bathrooms, fireplaces, and feature walls. Maintain minimalistic integrity by choosing understated finishes—honed or matte surfaces rather than overly polished or glossy treatments.

Glass: Clarity and Openness

Glass is the embodiment of minimalism's clarity, transparency, and openness. It visually expands spaces, enhances natural light, and introduces delicate elegance without clutter.

Choosing the Right Glass:
- Clear tempered glass maximizes visual transparency, while frosted or sandblasted glass adds subtle privacy while maintaining brightness.

Interior Applications:
- Employ glass for large windows, partitions, tabletops, shelving, and shower enclosures. Use glass sparingly but purposefully, ensuring each element contributes meaningfully to the overall design.

Textiles: Softness and Depth

Textiles provide essential softness, comfort, and acoustic balance. Fabrics like linen, wool, cotton, and silk introduce tactile interest, making minimalist interiors feel inviting rather than austere.

Selecting Textiles:
- Opt for high-quality, natural fibers. Linen and cotton offer breathable comfort and relaxed sophistication, wool brings warmth and texture, and silk lends quiet elegance.

Interior Applications:
- Textiles are best applied through upholstery, curtains, bedding, and decorative accessories such as rugs, cushions, and throws. Maintain neutral or muted palettes, allowing texture to provide depth rather than bold color contrasts.

Combining Essential Materials Harmoniously

Successful minimalist design often depends on the harmonious interplay of wood, stone, glass, and textiles. Here's how to achieve balance:

Contrast and Complement:
- Balance wood's warmth with stone's cool elegance, soften glass's sleekness with plush textiles, and complement textured stone surfaces with smooth wood finishes.

Consistency and Flow:
- Maintain visual continuity by repeating key materials across rooms. A thoughtful material palette enhances coherence and unity throughout your home.

Intentionality:
- Every material should have purpose—whether structural, functional, or aesthetic. Minimalism demands deliberate selection, ensuring each element meaningfully contributes to the overarching design philosophy.

Mastering these essential materials empowers you to craft minimalist spaces rich with sensory delight, authenticity, and elegant simplicity. Through thoughtful material selection and meticulous application, minimalism transforms your home into a refined, luxurious sanctuary—calm, balanced, and profoundly satisfying.

CHAPTER 2
THE ART OF THE MINIMALIST LIVING ROOM

Designing with Purpose and Simplicity

The living room stands at the heart of your home, a place where comfort, functionality, and style converge. When designed through the lens of minimalism, this space transforms into a serene haven defined by purposeful simplicity, each element contributing distinctly and intentionally to the overall harmony.

1. Defining Purpose in Your Living Room

The journey of designing a minimalist living room begins with clarity. Before choosing furnishings or decor, consider the primary purpose your living room serves. Whether it's relaxation, entertaining guests, family gatherings, or quiet reflection, identifying the core purpose guides all subsequent design choices.

Purposeful zoning:
- Divide your space subtly into functional zones—seating, conversation, media, reading—while maintaining fluid transitions. Minimalist design avoids unnecessary partitions, using subtle visual cues like rugs, furniture orientation, and lighting to delineate space without clutter.

2. Embracing Functional Simplicity

In minimalist design, simplicity equates directly to function. Every object in your living room should contribute meaningfully to its intended use and aesthetic balance.

Essential furniture only:
- Limit your selections to pieces that directly support the primary purpose. This usually includes seating, a coffee table, lighting, and possibly entertainment units or shelves. Each item must be chosen thoughtfully, emphasizing quality and longevity.

Streamlined storage solutions:
- Integrate hidden or seamlessly designed storage to maintain visual purity and prevent clutter accumulation. Built-in cabinetry or low-profile modular storage can effectively house essential items without sacrificing elegance.

3. Creating Visual Calmness and Clarity

Minimalism prioritizes visual tranquility. This requires careful balance and proportion within the living room.

Negative space:
- Celebrate emptiness as a meaningful design element. Leave space around furniture and decor, enabling visual rest and enhancing each item's individual presence.

Balanced proportions:
- Furniture and decor should relate proportionately both to each other and to the room itself. A large sofa in a small room or excessively small items in a spacious area can disrupt harmony. Measure carefully and visualize before placing furniture.

4. Integrating Natural Elements and Light

Natural elements and abundant lighting elevate minimalist interiors, adding warmth, depth, and freshness.

Natural light enhancement:
- Maximize daylight through expansive windows or strategically placed mirrors, minimizing heavy window treatments to ensure light flows freely.

Natural materials:
- Incorporate subtle natural textures—wood, linen, stone—to enrich sensory experience without clutter. Such materials inherently resonate with minimalist aesthetics, promoting tranquility and connection to nature.

5. Thoughtful Color and Texture Choices

Color and texture significantly influence minimalist environments. The living room should predominantly feature a neutral palette, but subtle textures enhance visual interest without sacrificing simplicity.

- Textural variety within neutrals:
- Utilize fabrics such as linen, wool, or textured rugs to create tactile interest. The nuanced interplay of different textures provides depth without visual chaos.

Controlled accents:
- If you introduce accent colors or metallic touches, apply them sparingly and consistently to maintain the overall cohesion of the minimalist approach.

6. Artistic and Decorative Intentionality

In minimalist living rooms, artwork and decorative elements hold significant visual and emotional weight. Carefully curated art becomes a focal point, adding personal expression without overwhelming the room.

Single focal points:
- Choose one or two key pieces of art or sculpture that meaningfully resonate with you, placing them thoughtfully to enhance the room's overall aesthetic.

Simplified decor:
- Keep decorative accessories to an absolute minimum—each object should carry emotional resonance or functional value, placed intentionally to complement rather than compete.

Designing a minimalist living room is a deliberate act of clarity, purpose, and restraint. Each choice, from furniture to lighting, from color to texture, must thoughtfully align to cultivate simplicity and elegance. The result is not merely a visually appealing space, but a living area that genuinely enhances your daily life, inspiring serenity and sophisticated simplicity with every glance.

Iconic Furniture Selection: From Sofas to Seating

In minimalist living rooms, each piece of furniture isn't merely functional—it becomes a statement of style and intention. Choosing iconic furnishings is essential; these pieces serve as visual anchors, setting the tone of quiet elegance and understated luxury throughout your space. Let's explore how to select iconic minimalist furniture, from sofas to accent seating, to create a cohesive, sophisticated aesthetic.

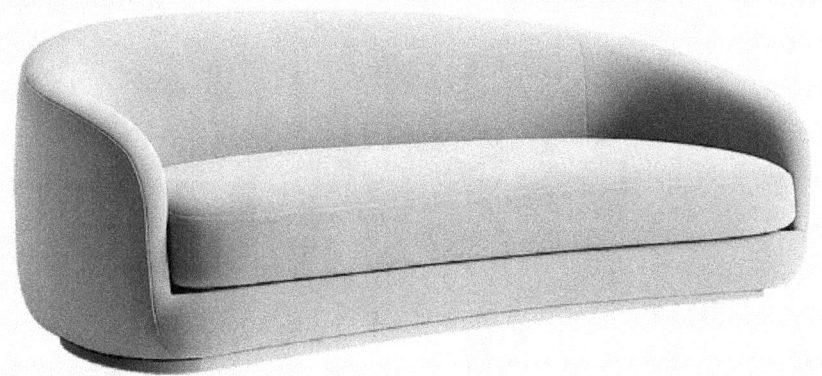

1. The Minimalist Sofa: Central to Comfort and Elegance

A sofa typically commands the focal point of any living room, making its selection crucial. Minimalist sofas should blend comfort, visual simplicity, and functional precision.

Form and Silhouette:
- Opt for sofas with clean lines, straight edges, and restrained detailing. Designs inspired by mid-century modern or contemporary European minimalism often perfectly balance form and function.

Size and Proportion:
- Carefully consider the sofa's scale relative to the room. It should be comfortably proportional, neither dominating the space nor appearing lost within it. Typical minimalist sofas are low-profile, visually unobtrusive, and spatially harmonious.

Material Choices:
- Select upholstery in premium natural fabrics like linen, cotton, wool, or leather, in neutral shades. These materials age gracefully, offering tactile pleasure and visual sophistication.

2. Selecting Complementary Seating

Additional seating options—such as lounge chairs, accent chairs, or benches—should complement rather than compete with the sofa. Each chair should be chosen for its unique character, enhancing your overall design narrative.

Iconic Chairs:
- Opt for seating with timeless appeal, such as mid-century classics or contemporary pieces characterized by simplicity and craftsmanship. Designs from iconic names like Hans Wegner, Charles and Ray Eames, or contemporary minimalist designers provide timeless appeal.

Mixing and Matching with Care:
- Maintain coherence through a unified design language (shape, color, texture). A curated mix of chairs creates interest without disrupting visual harmony. For instance, pairing a structured leather chair with a plush fabric sofa introduces subtle yet balanced contrast.

3. Essential Tables: Functional and Refined

Tables in minimalist interiors should appear effortlessly integrated. Coffee tables, side tables, and occasional tables should offer utility without visual heaviness.

Coffee Tables:
- Choose low, streamlined designs made from materials like wood, metal, or glass. Rectangular or round tables with sleek silhouettes foster visual flow and functional ease.

Side Tables and Occasional Tables:
- Use minimalistic designs—simple geometric shapes or slender forms—that blend subtly into the space. Consider transparency (glass or acrylic) or delicate frames for added visual lightness.

4. Purposeful Storage Pieces

Minimalism demands sophisticated storage solutions. Shelving and storage should integrate seamlessly, serving a clear purpose while reinforcing the visual clarity of the space.

Built-in or Modular Units:
- Select integrated or modular shelving systems with simple designs that reduce visual noise. Closed cabinetry keeps items discreetly out of sight, enhancing tranquility.

Multi-Functional Furniture:
- Consider pieces like storage benches or ottomans, combining practicality with elegance. These items discreetly support the minimalistic ethos by reducing clutter and maintaining visual harmony.

5. Timeless vs. Trendy Furniture Choices

Prioritizing timeless furniture ensures enduring aesthetic value, making your minimalist living room resilient to passing trends.

Invest in Iconic Quality:
- High-quality, timeless furniture might require greater initial investment but offers lasting aesthetic and practical value. Furniture designed by iconic minimalists remains stylishly relevant for decades.

Resist Trend-Based Purchases:
- Avoid fleeting styles that quickly lose appeal. Minimalism emphasizes longevity, durability, and timeless elegance, preserving visual coherence and sustainable consumption.

6. Craftsmanship and Detail

Attention to craftsmanship distinguishes minimalist furniture. Exceptional design, meticulous construction, and thoughtful detail transform ordinary furniture into extraordinary pieces.

Quality Craftsmanship:
- Evaluate furniture closely for construction integrity—joinery, upholstery finishes, stitching, and materials should be flawless.

Subtle Elegance:
- Minimalist furniture typically features discreet yet thoughtful details, such as refined joinery, minimal hardware, or subtle textural contrasts that enhance overall sophistication.

Selecting iconic furniture for your minimalist living room is an intentional process, guided by precision, restraint, and clarity. Each piece must earn its place in your space, embodying the elegance and purposeful simplicity intrinsic to minimalist luxury. Through careful selection, you'll create an interior that is timeless, harmonious, and uniquely personal, elevating everyday living into an exceptional experience.

Curating Spaciousness: Styling Without Clutter

Minimalist living rooms embody a profound sense of openness, inviting tranquility through intentional spaciousness. However, creating this feeling isn't simply about eliminating objects; it's about curating with meticulous intention. A carefully edited, uncluttered living room reflects purposeful elegance, allowing each element the room contains to shine genuinely.
Here's how to masterfully curate spaciousness while keeping your minimalist interior inviting and sophisticated.

1. Embracing Negative Space

Negative space—the empty areas surrounding furniture and decor—is central to minimalist interiors. Rather than seeing empty spaces as unfinished, recognize them as intentionally designed areas providing clarity and calmness.

Strategic Furniture Placement:
- Position furniture to maintain comfortable circulation paths, allowing visual breathing room. Leaving clear pathways and sufficient distances between pieces prevents crowding, emphasizing each item's intentional placement.

Avoiding Overcrowding:
- Resist the urge to fill corners or walls. Instead, let these empty spaces serve as restful intervals that enhance the visual impact of the selected furniture and decor.

2. Selecting Only Essential Decor

Every object placed in a minimalist living room must be considered and meaningful. The goal isn't mere sparsity but thoughtful selection.

One-In, One-Out Rule:
- Adopt this practice to maintain intentional curation. Whenever you introduce a new piece, evaluate if another should be removed, ensuring continued visual clarity.

Focus on Function and Beauty:
- Choose decor items that serve multiple roles: practical and aesthetic. A sculptural vase, for example, can function both as art and a vessel for fresh flowers.

3. Clever Storage and Hidden Solutions

Clutter is the enemy of minimalism. However, minimalist rooms still require practical storage. Thoughtful storage solutions can significantly contribute to spaciousness.

Hidden Storage:
- Employ built-in or recessed storage solutions that blend seamlessly into walls or furniture. Hidden compartments keep everyday items accessible yet unobtrusive.

Multifunctional Furniture:
- Furniture with integrated storage, such as coffee tables with hidden compartments or benches with lift-up seats, maximizes function without additional visual clutter.

4. Achieving Visual Harmony and Balance

Visual harmony is paramount in creating spaciousness. Each piece should contribute to an overall sense of balance.

Uniformity and Cohesion:
- Maintain consistency in color schemes, materials, and textures. Similar hues and textures unify the space, reducing visual fragmentation.

Scale and Proportion:
- Furniture should align proportionately with room size. Large items in small spaces or numerous small items in large rooms disrupt harmony. Opt for carefully scaled furnishings and decor that maintain visual balance.

5. Effective Use of Light and Mirrors

Lighting dramatically influences the perception of spaciousness. Strategic lighting choices can amplify space, while mirrors visually extend the room.

Natural Light Optimization:
- Maximize windows and reduce heavy treatments. Unobstructed natural light is vital, enhancing room openness significantly.

Mirrors as Visual Extenders:
- Place mirrors thoughtfully to reflect natural light and room views, multiplying perceived space without adding physical objects.

6. Artful Display and Minimalist Styling

Styling minimalist spaces requires restraint and clarity. Artistic display should be deliberately restrained, emphasizing visual simplicity and elegance.

Curated Art Placement:
- Limit displayed art to carefully selected pieces that resonate deeply, ideally one or two per room. Keep wall displays sparse, enhancing each artwork's individual impact.

Subtle Styling:
- Styling surfaces—such as shelves, tabletops, or mantels—should reflect intentional minimalism, often using singular or grouped objects carefully placed for visual tranquility.

7. Mindful Maintenance

Maintaining minimalism requires ongoing mindfulness, regularly evaluating your space to avoid gradual clutter build-up.

Regular Editing:
- Periodically assess your living room, removing items that no longer contribute positively or intentionally.

Commitment to Simplicity:
- Consistently favor simplicity and clarity, ensuring the space continually aligns with minimalist principles.

Curating spaciousness through purposeful minimalism isn't merely aesthetic—it's transformative. The resulting space becomes a tranquil retreat, a deliberate composition of simplicity, sophistication, and intentional living, making your home a sanctuary of refined elegance.

CHAPTER 3
DINING SPACES DEFINED BY SIMPLICITY

Less Furniture, Maximum Impact

In a minimalist dining space, elegance is achieved not by abundance, but through thoughtful selection and refined restraint. The goal is to craft an environment where every item has purpose and meaning, balancing aesthetics with functionality to create a visually harmonious and emotionally satisfying space. A well-curated minimalist dining room evokes serenity and sophistication. Each carefully chosen piece should effortlessly embody the room's aesthetic philosophy—quality, craftsmanship, and timeless elegance—while enhancing the experience of dining itself.

The Art of Intentional Furniture Selection

Minimalism does not equate to emptiness. Rather, it's about choosing furniture thoughtfully and with clear intent. Begin by identifying precisely what your dining area requires: typically, this includes a table, seating, and perhaps a discreet storage solution. Selecting fewer pieces allows each item to shine individually and collectively enhance the overall composition.

Anchor with the Perfect Table
- The dining table is the natural centerpiece. Select a table defined by simplicity of form, proportion, and fine craftsmanship. High-quality materials—solid wood, marble, polished concrete, or tempered glass—naturally embody minimalist sophistication. A clean-lined rectangular table sets a structured tone, while round or oval shapes create a sense of ease and intimacy.

Complementary Seating Choices
- Chairs should reflect the table's elegance but provide a subtle contrast. Consider chairs with streamlined forms, minimal detailing, and subtle yet inviting upholstery. Comfort is crucial—minimalism doesn't forsake practicality for aesthetics. Ergonomic chairs that blend seamlessly with the dining table create a visually coherent, inviting dining experience.

Creating Visual Clarity and Openness

Clarity is essential to minimalist design. By strategically positioning furniture and allowing generous spaces between items, the dining area achieves an inviting openness. Avoid overcrowding or excessive visual stimuli. Embrace negative space—the deliberate, intentional gaps between objects—as a powerful design feature, fostering tranquility and ease of movement around the dining area.

Spatial Balance and Harmony
- Consider the proportions of your furniture carefully. Oversized pieces can dominate and overwhelm the space, while items too small might appear lost or insignificant. Balance is key—select furniture proportional to the room's dimensions and consider furniture height and volume in relation to ceiling heights and room widths.

Thoughtful Placement
- Position furniture to enhance flow and encourage comfortable social interactions. Adequate space around chairs ensures ease of movement and visual breathing room, subtly elevating comfort and functionality without sacrificing style.

Elegant Storage Solutions

Minimalism relies on discreet yet highly functional storage options. Cabinets, sideboards, or integrated shelving systems should seamlessly blend into your dining area's aesthetic, offering storage without compromising the spaciousness.

Invisible Yet Accessible
- Choose storage solutions that become part of the room rather than separate entities—cabinets matching wall colors or finishes that recede visually, keeping necessary items hidden but conveniently accessible.

Multifunctional Elegance
- Sideboards or consoles can double as serving surfaces and decorative platforms, further consolidating function while preserving minimalism's visual clarity. Such pieces should mirror the aesthetic principles of your table and chairs, maintaining consistency and elegance throughout the room.

Styling with Purpose

Decorative elements in minimalist dining rooms should be carefully chosen, limited, and purposeful. Each decorative piece should significantly enhance the ambiance without overwhelming or distracting attention from the furniture.

Singular Decorative Focus
- Opt for singular, impactful pieces—a sculptural centerpiece, carefully selected ceramics, or thoughtfully curated art. Each item should feel like a deliberate choice, effortlessly blending functionality and aesthetics.

Thoughtful Art Display
- Art in minimalist spaces must resonate deeply. A single large canvas, carefully positioned, or a thoughtfully placed sculpture creates impact without clutter. Keep decorative styling restrained and intentional, ensuring each object holds personal significance.

Materials and Textures for Subtle Impact

Minimalist dining rooms rely on materials and textures to provide visual depth without clutter. Incorporate subtle textures—softly grained woods, smooth marble surfaces, matte ceramics, or luxurious yet simple textiles—to infuse depth and tactile interest subtly.

Layering Textures
- Introduce depth through careful layering: a sleek wood table against softly upholstered chairs, paired with smooth ceramic tableware. Texture, rather than abundance, creates a sophisticated sensory experience.

Unified Palette
- Keep color schemes refined, restrained, and consistent. Neutral, muted tones unify the space, emphasizing craftsmanship, form, and the natural beauty of materials.

By consciously embracing fewer, higher-quality furnishings, your minimalist dining area becomes an elegant testament to the power of intentional living. Each piece becomes meaningful and significant, offering a profound, sensory-rich experience every time you gather around the table.

Lighting to Enhance Dining Ambience

In a minimalist dining room, lighting does more than illuminate—it shapes the mood, emphasizes the elegance of simplicity, and subtly enhances the entire experience of dining. Thoughtfully designed lighting solutions can completely transform a space, accentuating its finest qualities and providing the perfect atmosphere for both everyday meals and special occasions.

Crafting Mood with Purposeful Lighting

Lighting in a minimalist space should feel intentional yet effortless. Every fixture must serve a clear purpose, seamlessly integrating with the room's overall aesthetic while providing functional illumination. The goal is to combine practicality with elegance, creating an inviting atmosphere that feels calm, balanced, and refined.

Layered Lighting for Comfort and Flexibility
- Minimalism benefits greatly from a multi-layered lighting approach. Incorporating ambient, task, and accent lighting allows you to effortlessly adapt the space according to mood, occasion, and need. Ambient lighting gently illuminates the entire room, while targeted task lighting ensures functional clarity for dining. Accent lights highlight specific focal points—such as a beautiful piece of art or an architectural detail—without cluttering the visual landscape.

Choosing the Perfect Fixture

A minimalist dining area often revolves around a single, carefully selected lighting fixture that becomes the focal point of the room. The right fixture provides illumination while reinforcing your overall design philosophy.

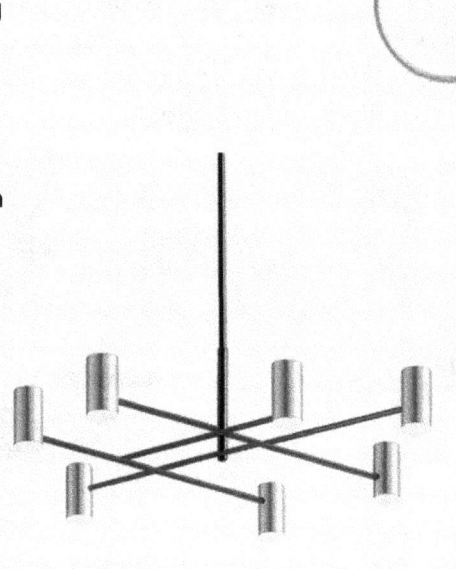

Sculptural Simplicity
- Select lighting fixtures characterized by clean lines, elegant forms, and understated craftsmanship. Pendants, chandeliers, or linear lights with minimal detailing ensure visual purity, offering subtle yet impactful design statements.

Scale and Proportion
- Proportion is critical. A large, sculptural pendant light can beautifully anchor a dining table, providing a visual center point without overwhelming the room. Conversely, overly small fixtures may diminish the impact, resulting in a lack of visual coherence. Carefully match fixture size with table proportions and ceiling height.

Utilizing Natural Light to Elevate the Space

Natural light plays an essential role in minimalist design. It brings warmth, clarity, and freshness into your dining area, enhancing the beauty of textures and colors without additional visual distractions.

Maximizing Daylight

- Encourage natural light flow with minimal window treatments—sheer curtains, blinds, or unobtrusive window shades. The daylight will soften your space, highlighting the elegance of furnishings and the simplicity of design.

Balancing Daylight with Artificial Lighting

- Artificial lighting should seamlessly supplement natural daylight. Opt for dimmable fixtures to adjust illumination effortlessly, maintaining a harmonious balance throughout the day and into the evening.

Accentuating Materials and Textures

Minimalist interiors rely heavily on carefully chosen materials and subtle textures. Proper lighting accentuates these elements, drawing attention to their intrinsic beauty without overwhelming the senses.

Directional Accent Lighting

- Employ subtle spotlights or wall sconces to highlight textures—such as natural stone surfaces, sleek wooden tables, or elegantly upholstered chairs. These targeted accents enhance depth and interest without compromising visual clarity.

Warm vs. Cool Lighting

- Choose lighting temperature intentionally. Warm light sources create an inviting, comfortable atmosphere ideal for dining, highlighting the richness of natural materials. Cooler lighting tones can enhance crisp, clean aesthetics but should be used sparingly to maintain a welcoming ambiance.

Sustainable and Smart Lighting Solutions

Sustainability is inherently aligned with minimalist values—less waste, greater efficiency, intentional living. Incorporating sustainable lighting solutions enhances the functionality, elegance, and ethics of your dining area.

Energy-Efficient Fixtures
- Opt for LED lighting, which provides excellent illumination quality, flexibility in color temperature, and significantly reduced energy consumption compared to traditional lighting solutions.

Smart Controls and Dimmers
- Incorporate smart lighting systems that allow easy adjustment of brightness levels, color temperatures, and lighting zones. Automated or voice-controlled lighting can effortlessly set scenes for different dining experiences, from intimate dinners to lively gatherings.

Final Reflections on Minimalist Lighting

Lighting in a minimalist dining room requires thoughtful balance and nuanced design. When chosen intentionally, lighting fixtures and techniques significantly enhance the dining experience, creating spaces that are at once refined, comfortable, and deeply satisfying.

Remember, minimalism isn't about reducing for the sake of emptiness; it's about elevating each element to its highest potential. Thoughtful lighting embodies this principle beautifully, setting a refined tone, drawing attention to intentional details, and enriching every moment spent at the dining table.

CHAPTER 4
SERENE BEDROOMS

Creating a Tranquil Sleeping Sanctuary

Your bedroom is more than simply a room for rest—it is a sanctuary, a place of calm, restoration, and peace. A minimalist bedroom thoughtfully merges simplicity with comfort, providing a serene refuge from the world's chaos. Creating such a sanctuary involves careful attention to every detail, ensuring that your space invites restfulness and tranquility through deliberate and elegant design choices.

Designing for Serenity

The first step in crafting a tranquil sleeping sanctuary is understanding what serenity means to you. Minimalism is personal; your bedroom must reflect your unique preferences while adhering to principles of intentional simplicity. Begin by defining the atmosphere you desire—peaceful, soft, airy, or cozy—and build your design choices around these emotional anchors.

Embrace Simplicity in Furniture Choices

Minimalist bedroom furniture should exude quiet elegance and understated functionality. Furniture pieces such as your bed frame, bedside tables, and storage should not overwhelm the space. Instead, they should create harmony, enhancing the peaceful ambiance without visual distractions.

The Bed as a Centerpiece
- The bed is undoubtedly the room's focal point. Opt for a sleek, well-crafted bed frame with clean lines, minimal detailing, and high-quality materials such as solid wood, natural upholstery, or subtle metallic finishes. Low-profile beds reinforce a sense of spaciousness and relaxation.

Streamlined Bedside Tables
- Bedside tables should be both visually unobtrusive and functional. Choose designs with minimal detailing—perhaps simple wooden or metal tables with a single drawer or shelf to reduce clutter and encourage visual calmness.

Color Palettes for Calmness

Color is vital in influencing mood and tranquility. Minimalist bedrooms thrive on soft, neutral palettes that promote restful relaxation and a sense of serenity.

Neutral Elegance
- Select soothing shades such as soft whites, muted creams, pale grays, or subtle earth tones. These colors create an inviting and calm ambiance, perfectly supporting restful sleep.

Subtle Contrasts
- Introduce subtle contrasts to maintain visual interest without disrupting serenity. Soft tonal variations or gentle textural differences can enrich the overall visual experience while preserving tranquility.

Integrating Natural Elements

Nature and minimalism inherently complement each other. Incorporating natural elements such as wood, stone, plants, or organic fabrics fosters a deep sense of calm and grounding.

Natural Textures
- Wood flooring, stone accents, or linen textiles can significantly enhance sensory comfort. These materials convey authenticity and warmth, creating a tactile richness within the simplicity.

Plants for Freshness
- Select a few carefully placed plants known for their calming properties and air-purifying qualities, such as peace lilies or snake plants. Plants gently infuse life and softness, further enriching your sleeping sanctuary.

Decluttering for Mental Clarity

A tranquil sleeping sanctuary must be free of clutter—visual or physical. Excess items, unnecessary decor, and disorganized storage disrupt mental clarity and hinder relaxation. Effective decluttering transforms your bedroom into a serene, restorative environment.

Hidden Storage Solutions
- Utilize discreet storage—built-in wardrobes, under-bed drawers, or minimalist storage benches—to keep personal belongings organized yet hidden from view.

Consistent Maintenance
- Regularly reassess your space, removing items that no longer serve a clear purpose or enhance your experience. This practice ensures continued serenity and clarity.

Textures for Tactile Comfort

Minimalist bedrooms greatly benefit from the thoughtful layering of textures. Incorporating soft fabrics, plush rugs, and smooth surfaces creates sensory comfort that invites restfulness without visual overload.

Layered Bedding and Textiles
- Carefully select bedding with calming textures and softness. Linen, cotton, wool, and cashmere fabrics contribute to a tactile experience that enhances relaxation and comfort.

Soft Flooring Choices
- Soft rugs or natural flooring materials, like wool carpets or textured wooden flooring, enhance warmth and comfort underfoot, amplifying the sense of tranquility in the room.

Lighting for Calm Ambience

Lighting profoundly influences bedroom tranquility. Soft, layered lighting solutions that include ambient, task, and accent lighting create an adaptable, serene atmosphere.

Soft Ambient Lighting
- Use gentle, diffused lighting through sconces, floor lamps, or dimmable fixtures. These soften the atmosphere, fostering relaxation as evening arrives.

Control of Natural Light
- Balance natural daylight with the use of sheer curtains or minimal window treatments to control brightness, creating gentle illumination that enhances serenity.

Personal Touches with Purpose

Minimalism does not imply coldness or impersonality. On the contrary, carefully selected personal items deepen emotional connections with your bedroom. Select meaningful items—perhaps one piece of cherished artwork or a few treasured photographs—that resonate deeply with you. Display these intentionally, enhancing emotional comfort without compromising the minimalist ethos.

Ultimately, creating a tranquil sleeping sanctuary is about achieving harmonious balance. By carefully curating furniture, thoughtfully selecting color palettes, integrating natural elements, and intentionally managing clutter, you transform your bedroom into an oasis of serenity—inviting restfulness, encouraging reflection, and nurturing the peacefulness essential for genuine rejuvenation.

Bedding and Textiles: Comfort Meets Elegance

In a minimalist bedroom, textiles are the gentle touch that transforms simplicity into genuine comfort. Bedding and textiles not only define the aesthetic elegance of your sleeping sanctuary but directly influence the quality of your sleep and overall sense of well-being. Carefully selecting fabrics, textures, and subtle color variations ensures your space exudes calm sophistication without sacrificing luxurious comfort.

Choosing the Right Bedding

Bedding anchors the experience of your bedroom—it's the first thing you touch as you wake and the last comfort you experience before sleep. Selecting bedding thoughtfully means balancing aesthetic simplicity with tactile comfort.

Fabric Selection: A Sensory Experience

Linen: Highly breathable, natural linen is a staple in minimalist bedrooms. Its relaxed texture softens with each wash, enhancing comfort and lending a casual elegance.

Cotton: Premium cotton, especially Egyptian or Supima, offers exceptional softness, durability, and a crisp, refined feel. Cotton's breathability makes it perfect for all seasons.

Silk and Satin: Offering an understated luxury, silk or satin bedding introduces subtle glamour. Their smooth textures are gentle against the skin, providing comfort that feels indulgent yet refined.

Colors and Patterns: Quiet Sophistication

- Stick with neutral palettes such as whites, soft grays, muted earth tones, or delicate pastels. These shades reinforce tranquility, creating visual calmness conducive to restful sleep.
- Minimalist design typically avoids complex patterns. If patterns are used, opt for subtle, barely-there textures or discreet tonal variations. Quiet sophistication ensures visual interest without disrupting serenity.

Layering for Depth and Warmth

Minimalist bedrooms greatly benefit from strategic layering of textiles. Proper layering contributes not only to aesthetic elegance but also practical comfort and tactile luxury.

Duvets, Quilts, and Blankets
- Select a high-quality duvet in neutral shades, filled with down, wool, or hypoallergenic alternatives. Duvets should feel light yet warm, offering cozy comfort without visual heaviness.
- Layer quilts or blankets subtly. Choose these in complementary shades, ensuring they enhance depth without overwhelming simplicity.

Accent Throws
- A single luxurious throw, such as a cashmere or wool blanket at the foot of the bed, provides an elegant finish. This simple addition elevates warmth, inviting relaxation and subtly enhancing visual interest.

Pillows: Functional Comfort and Visual Harmony

Pillows in minimalist bedrooms are both practical and decorative. Their careful selection enhances comfort, supports sleep quality, and reinforces the bedroom's aesthetic coherence.

- Functional Pillows: Opt for supportive, comfortable sleeping pillows in high-quality materials such as memory foam, down, or natural latex. Comfort remains paramount in minimalist design.
- Decorative Pillows: Limit decorative pillows to one or two carefully selected items, chosen for their subtle texture, muted color palette, or elegant simplicity. These pillows enhance the aesthetic without cluttering the visual landscape.

Rugs and Floor Textiles

The tactile experience of a bedroom extends beyond the bed itself. Rugs and floor textiles subtly influence warmth, comfort, and overall sensory richness.

- Natural Rugs: Rugs crafted from wool, cotton, jute, or sisal integrate beautifully into minimalist spaces. These materials lend warmth and texture, complementing the room's calm aesthetics.
- Placement and Size: Choose generously sized rugs placed under the bed to ground the space, creating an inviting visual unity. Smaller accent rugs can also define specific areas, such as a reading nook or seating area, providing tactile and visual comfort.

Window Treatments: Elegance with Simplicity

Window treatments in minimalist bedrooms should balance functionality—privacy, light control, insulation—with visual elegance.

- Sheer and Lightweight Fabrics: Sheer curtains or softly textured linens let natural light gently filter through, reinforcing the bedroom's airy, calm atmosphere.
- Minimal Hardware and Design: Select streamlined hardware, subtle curtain rods, or integrated roller blinds. Avoid elaborate drapery, favoring simplicity to maintain visual serenity.

Sustainable and Ethical Choices

Minimalist philosophy often aligns with sustainability, emphasizing conscious, ethical choices that respect both your home and the planet.

- Opt for organic, sustainably sourced textiles, free from harmful chemicals. Organic linen, cotton, or wool provides comfort, durability, and ecological responsibility.
- Consider textiles crafted by fair trade and ethical manufacturers. Such choices enhance the comfort of your bedroom and promote responsible living.

Maintaining Elegance and Comfort

Proper care preserves the beauty, comfort, and longevity of your chosen textiles:

- Regularly launder bedding with gentle detergents and cold water to maintain softness and color integrity.
- Rotate and refresh bedding regularly, investing in durable, high-quality pieces that age gracefully, maintaining their elegance and comfort over time.

Textiles in a minimalist bedroom offer a uniquely sensory experience—visual simplicity coupled with tactile indulgence. When thoughtfully selected, each fabric enhances comfort, provides luxurious warmth, and contributes subtly yet significantly to the bedroom's serene atmosphere. The careful interplay of textiles transforms your sleeping sanctuary into a truly comforting and elegant retreat.

Ambient Lighting for Peaceful Rest

Lighting profoundly shapes the mood and ambiance of your bedroom, directly impacting your ability to relax, unwind, and rest. In minimalist bedrooms, the thoughtful use of ambient lighting is crucial, as it provides a soft, soothing atmosphere that effortlessly transitions your space from day to night. Effective lighting creates a nurturing environment conducive to peaceful sleep and gentle awakening, reinforcing the serene simplicity central to minimalist design.

Setting the Mood with Soft Illumination

The primary goal of ambient lighting in minimalist bedrooms is to achieve a delicate balance between functional visibility and restful comfort. Rather than strong, direct light sources, ambient lighting emphasizes subtlety and diffusion, providing a gentle glow that envelops the room without harshness or visual strain.

Soft Diffusion:
- Opt for fixtures or lamps with frosted, translucent, or fabric shades that soften and disperse light. This diffused glow gently illuminates the entire room, supporting a peaceful and calming environment conducive to sleep.

Warm vs. Cool Light Temperatures:
- Warm-toned lighting (2700K to 3000K) is ideal for bedrooms, promoting relaxation and reducing eye strain. Avoid cool white or blue-toned lights in bedrooms, as these can stimulate alertness and interfere with sleep.

Layered Lighting for Flexibility

Successful ambient lighting in minimalist bedrooms involves layering multiple light sources, allowing flexibility to adjust brightness according to your specific needs or preferences throughout the day.

Primary Ambient Lighting:
- Ceiling fixtures, pendant lamps, or subtle recessed lighting serve as primary ambient sources, softly illuminating the room without creating stark shadows or overly bright spots.

Secondary Sources for Softness:
- Complement primary lighting with secondary sources such as table lamps, floor lamps, or wall sconces. These smaller fixtures offer additional warmth and intimacy, perfect for quiet reading or winding down before sleep.

Dimmer Controls:
- Incorporating dimmers or smart lighting systems enables precise adjustments of brightness levels. This flexibility lets you effortlessly transition from brighter daytime settings to dim, restful evening lighting.

Integrating Natural and Artificial Lighting

Natural light significantly influences your bedroom's ambience. Skillfully balancing artificial and natural sources ensures harmonious lighting throughout the day, enhancing the minimalist room's clarity and tranquility.

Maximizing Natural Daylight:
- Minimal window treatments such as sheer curtains or subtle blinds allow gentle, diffused sunlight to illuminate your bedroom softly. Natural daylight enhances emotional well-being, provides visual comfort, and elevates your bedroom's serene atmosphere.

Evening Transitions:
- Use artificial lighting strategically as daylight fades. Gradually dim artificial sources as evening approaches, seamlessly transitioning your bedroom from vibrant daytime brightness to tranquil nighttime calmness.

Lighting Placement for Serenity and Functionality

Thoughtful placement of lighting fixtures significantly enhances the restful quality of your minimalist bedroom. Careful positioning ensures visual comfort, practical functionality, and atmospheric elegance.

Bedside Lighting:
- Install subtle bedside lights that provide gentle illumination for reading or relaxation. Wall-mounted sconces or minimalist table lamps are particularly suitable, freeing up surfaces and maintaining visual simplicity.

Accent Lighting:
- Employ discreet accent lights to highlight calming design elements, such as textured walls, artwork, or plants. The goal is subtlety, creating points of visual interest without disrupting the serene aesthetic.

Indirect Illumination:
- Utilize indirect lighting techniques, such as LED strips concealed behind headboards or within architectural features, to softly illuminate the room without harsh direct glare. Indirect lighting emphasizes tranquility, creating a cozy, enveloping glow.

Selecting Fixtures for Minimalist Elegance

Lighting fixtures in minimalist bedrooms should reflect simplicity, elegance, and understated beauty. Each fixture serves both practical and aesthetic roles, complementing the room's serene atmosphere without visual distraction.

Simplified Design:
- Choose fixtures with minimal detailing, clean lines, and refined finishes. Subtle metallics, matte textures, or natural materials harmonize seamlessly with minimalist interiors.

Fixture Scale and Proportion:
- Ensure lighting fixtures are proportionate to your room's dimensions and furnishings. Fixtures that are too large or elaborate may overwhelm visual harmony, while excessively small lights might lack the desired visual impact.

Mindful Lighting for Enhanced Sleep Quality

Ambient lighting choices directly influence sleep quality, circadian rhythms, and overall well-being. Mindful lighting strategies facilitate a deeper, more restful sleep and a gentle, restorative awakening.

Pre-Sleep Illumination:
- Gradually reduce lighting levels as bedtime approaches, signaling your body that it's time to unwind. Warm, dimmed lighting helps reduce stress and promotes melatonin production, supporting restful sleep.

Morning Gentle Awakening:
- Employ soft, gradual lighting to gently ease you into the day. Natural daylight or gentle ambient illumination can create a more comfortable waking experience compared to abrupt, bright lighting.

Final Reflections

The thoughtful design of ambient lighting significantly transforms your minimalist bedroom into a genuinely restful sanctuary. Through careful selection, intentional layering, and mindful placement, lighting not only complements but elevates the entire experience of your sleeping environment, fostering peaceful rest, enhancing relaxation, and nurturing emotional well-being.

CHAPTER 5
EFFORTLESSLY
MINIMALIST
KITCHENS

Achieving an Uncluttered Kitchen Space

The kitchen is often described as the heart of the home—a space filled with life, activity, and warmth. However, this vitality can easily give way to clutter, creating visual and emotional stress. Minimalist kitchens, in contrast, are defined by a sense of effortless calm and spaciousness. Achieving an uncluttered kitchen space isn't simply about cleanliness or organization— it's a carefully curated balance of aesthetics, function, and intentionality.

Intentional Kitchen Planning

Creating an uncluttered kitchen begins with strategic planning. The layout and structure of your kitchen should support functionality without unnecessary visual complexity.

Functional Zoning
- Divide your kitchen into clearly defined zones for preparation, cooking, storage, and cleanup. Each area should logically flow into the next, minimizing unnecessary movement and visual chaos.

Streamlined Workflow
- Optimize your kitchen layout— whether a classic triangle (fridge, stove, sink) or an intuitive, linear design. Minimizing movement between key tasks helps maintain order, efficiency, and visual simplicity.

Embracing Minimalist Storage Solutions

Effective storage solutions are pivotal to maintaining an uncluttered kitchen. Storage should integrate seamlessly into the kitchen design, ensuring every item has its designated place.

Integrated Cabinetry
- Opt for cabinets designed to blend seamlessly into walls or surrounding architecture. Concealed hardware, handle-less designs, and built-in shelving enhance visual continuity and maintain sleek simplicity.

Smart Organization Within Cabinets
- Internal organization is equally important. Incorporate intelligent solutions like pull-out drawers, custom shelving, and concealed compartments to optimize space and accessibility.

Reducing Visual Noise

A truly minimalist kitchen significantly reduces visual distractions, promoting a sense of calm and openness.

Cleared Countertops
- Keep countertops clear by storing appliances and kitchen tools out of sight or neatly hidden. If necessary, limit visible items to carefully chosen objects that contribute aesthetically and practically, such as a stylish kettle or a beautifully simple fruit bowl.

Consistent Color and Materials
- Select materials and finishes that unify your kitchen visually. Uniform colors and minimal textural contrasts help create a cohesive, peaceful environment, reducing visual fragmentation.

Curating Essential Appliances

Minimalist kitchens rely on carefully curated appliances. Selecting fewer, multifunctional, and aesthetically cohesive appliances reinforces clarity, simplicity, and functionality.

Multifunctional Appliances
- Choose appliances that perform multiple tasks efficiently, reducing the need for numerous separate gadgets. For instance, combination ovens or integrated coffee makers streamline functionality without additional clutter.

Integrated Appliances
- Built-in refrigerators, dishwashers, and microwaves blend effortlessly with cabinetry, reinforcing visual harmony and promoting an uncluttered aesthetic.

Thoughtful Use of Open Shelving

While open shelving can create a minimalist aesthetic, it must be executed thoughtfully to avoid visual clutter.

Selective Display
- Carefully curate what is displayed—perhaps simple ceramics, consistent glassware, or elegant cookware—maintaining visual unity and functional accessibility without overcrowding.

Balance and Placement
- Open shelving should balance enclosed cabinetry, placed strategically to enhance visual openness without compromising simplicity.

Sophisticated Cabinetry and Functional Appliances

In a minimalist kitchen, cabinetry and appliances form the structural backbone of design—elements that must blend aesthetic elegance with streamlined functionality. Sophisticated cabinetry and thoughtfully selected appliances not only enhance visual harmony but significantly improve usability, ensuring every interaction within your kitchen feels intuitive, enjoyable, and effortlessly elegant.

Cabinetry: The Foundation of Minimalist Sophistication

Minimalist cabinetry goes beyond simple storage—it provides a visual anchor, shaping the aesthetic identity of your kitchen. Sophisticated cabinetry choices reflect impeccable craftsmanship, subtle elegance, and meticulous attention to detail.

Seamless Integration
- Cabinetry in minimalist kitchens often integrates seamlessly into walls, appearing almost as architectural features rather than separate furniture. Flush, handle-less cabinets or subtle, recessed pulls create smooth, uninterrupted surfaces, significantly reducing visual clutter.

Quality Craftsmanship
- Exceptional craftsmanship is critical in minimalist cabinetry. Each cabinet should demonstrate precise joinery, flawless finishes, and impeccable alignment. The subtle elegance of perfectly fitted cabinetry enhances the minimalist aesthetic while promoting lasting durability.

Consistent Material Choices
- Cabinet materials should harmonize with your overall kitchen design. Solid woods, matte or satin lacquered finishes, natural veneers, or smooth laminates offer understated sophistication. Consistent materials create visual cohesion and reinforce an overall sense of harmony.

Functional and Efficient Interior Organization

Sophisticated cabinetry extends beyond external appearance—it must offer exceptional interior functionality. Thoughtful internal organization ensures your kitchen remains both aesthetically pleasing and highly efficient.

Customized Storage Solutions
- Incorporate specialized storage solutions—such as pull-out shelves, internal organizers, spice racks, integrated trash bins, and dedicated compartments for pots, pans, or utensils—to maintain effortless order. These features maximize space efficiency while minimizing visual disruption.

Concealed Storage
- Hidden drawers, built-in compartments, and recessed shelves discreetly store appliances, cookware, and utensils, preserving visual clarity. Concealed storage solutions enable easy access to essentials without sacrificing aesthetic refinement.

Selecting Functional Appliances

Appliances in minimalist kitchens must align seamlessly with cabinetry, ensuring cohesive aesthetics and optimal functionality. Each appliance should blend subtly yet distinctly into the kitchen's visual landscape, offering intuitive usability without visual clutter.

Built-In Appliances
- Built-in ovens, refrigerators, dishwashers, and microwaves maintain visual continuity by integrating flawlessly into cabinetry. Paneled appliances (with matching cabinetry fronts) or sleek stainless steel designs create harmonious aesthetics, ensuring appliances remain unobtrusive.

Multifunctional Design
- Prioritize multifunctional appliances that perform several tasks efficiently. Combination ovens, steam ovens, induction cooktops with integrated extraction systems, or refrigerators with multiple climate zones significantly reduce the need for multiple separate appliances, reinforcing minimalist clarity.

Quality and Efficiency
- Invest in high-quality, energy-efficient appliances designed to offer exceptional performance, reliability, and sustainability. Premium appliances provide lasting value, minimal maintenance, and consistently superior functionality.

Balancing Technology and Minimalism

Modern minimalist kitchens benefit greatly from integrating advanced technologies subtly yet effectively. Technology must enhance functionality without disrupting visual serenity or creating unnecessary complexity.

Intelligent Appliances
- Select smart appliances that offer streamlined, intuitive interfaces, digital controls, or voice-enabled interactions. The goal is seamless operation, offering efficiency without unnecessary visual or functional complexity.

Subtle Digital Integration
- Digital displays, if visible, should remain unobtrusive, streamlined, and minimally noticeable. Alternatively, consider appliances with integrated, hidden interfaces that activate only when needed, preserving visual tranquility.

Finishes and Textures: Refined Sophistication

Finishes and textures significantly influence the kitchen's aesthetic experience. Choose cabinetry and appliance finishes that exude sophistication, reinforce visual coherence, and subtly enhance the room's tactile and visual depth.

Matte and Satin Finishes
- Matte and satin finishes offer refined sophistication, reducing glare and promoting visual calmness. Soft-touch cabinetry surfaces or muted metallic appliance finishes create a soothing visual landscape, enhancing minimalist aesthetics.

Textural Consistency
- Maintain consistency in cabinetry and appliance finishes to reinforce visual harmony. Subtle variations—such as matte cabinetry paired with polished metallic handles or glass surfaces—can add gentle visual interest without compromising simplicity.

Maintenance and Durability

Sophisticated minimalist kitchens require thoughtful consideration of long-term durability and ease of maintenance:

- Durable Materials: Prioritize robust, high-quality materials that withstand daily use without significant wear or degradation.
- Easy-to-Clean Surfaces: Choose finishes and surfaces that facilitate quick, effortless cleaning, maintaining the pristine simplicity essential to minimalist aesthetics.

Final Reflections

Sophisticated cabinetry and thoughtfully selected appliances form the core of a minimalist kitchen's elegant functionality. By carefully choosing seamless integration, exceptional craftsmanship, multifunctional appliances, and refined finishes, you cultivate a kitchen environment that feels effortlessly luxurious, intuitively functional, and consistently serene. Every aspect of your kitchen, from cabinetry to appliances, should reflect the mindful simplicity and subtle sophistication central to minimalist design—transforming everyday activities into deeply enjoyable, peaceful experiences.

Warmth Through Natural Textures

A common misconception about minimalist kitchens is that they must feel stark or overly clinical. However, successful minimalism is anything but cold—it intentionally incorporates warmth, depth, and tactile richness through carefully chosen natural textures. By thoughtfully integrating wood, stone, textiles, and organic materials, your minimalist kitchen becomes not only visually inviting but emotionally comforting, balancing visual simplicity with sensory warmth.

The Importance of Texture in Minimalism

In minimalist spaces, texture serves as an essential tool, subtly enriching the visual experience without overwhelming the aesthetic purity. Natural textures create warmth, depth, and dimension, adding interest to otherwise streamlined interiors.

- Visual Comfort: Textures soften the sharp edges of minimalist design, creating an inviting, approachable space.
- Tactile Pleasure: Natural textures engage the senses, providing tactile comfort and enhancing everyday interactions within your kitchen.

Wood: Organic Warmth and Timeless Elegance

Wood is foundational to creating warmth in minimalist kitchens. Its natural grain, subtle color variations, and organic character introduce authenticity and coziness, effortlessly balancing minimalism's inherent simplicity.

- Cabinetry and Shelving: Incorporating wooden cabinetry or open shelving adds immediate warmth. Woods like oak, walnut, or birch offer distinct grain patterns and tones that enrich visual interest while maintaining elegance.
- Countertops and Flooring: Wood countertops or flooring deliver consistent tactile warmth, enhancing visual continuity and grounding the kitchen's aesthetic.

Stone: Earthy Depth and Subtle Elegance

Natural stone brings enduring elegance, depth, and subtle sophistication. Each stone surface introduces unique patterns, colors, and textures, providing a luxurious yet understated warmth.

- Countertops and Islands: Marble, quartzite, soapstone, or granite countertops offer refined sophistication. The subtle veining and soft natural hues of these stones provide visual warmth and depth.
- Backsplashes and Accents: Stone backsplashes or carefully placed accents add visual richness without cluttering the aesthetic, emphasizing timeless beauty.

Natural Fabrics and Textiles

Introducing textiles into your minimalist kitchen provides softness, comfort, and warmth, creating sensory richness without disrupting the visual calmness.

- Curtains and Window Treatments: Soft, natural fabrics like linen or cotton gently filter daylight, contributing subtle texture and warmth.
- Rugs and Seating: Textured rugs or upholstered seating enhance tactile comfort, adding warmth underfoot and inviting visual softness. Choose muted, natural tones to harmonize with minimalist aesthetics.

Ceramics and Clay: Artisanal Elegance

Ceramic and clay items introduce subtle, handcrafted beauty, adding depth and personality to minimalist kitchens. The inherent imperfections and nuanced textures of ceramics provide gentle warmth and authenticity.

- Tableware and Decorative Objects: Handcrafted ceramic bowls, vases, or serving dishes elegantly combine function and aesthetics, introducing natural warmth.
- Tile Accents: Carefully selected ceramic tile backsplashes or accent walls add understated visual interest and texture without overwhelming the design.

Glass and Metallic Accents

Subtle metallic or glass textures introduce gentle warmth and reflectivity, enhancing the kitchen's visual depth without compromising minimalist simplicity.

- Warm Metallic Finishes: Brass, copper, or bronze fixtures, hardware, or small decorative touches provide warmth and sophistication. These materials gently reflect light, adding subtle visual interest.
- Textured Glass: Frosted or textured glass cabinet doors or decorative elements soften visual austerity, providing subtle tactile and visual warmth.

Balancing Textural Harmony

Incorporating natural textures successfully involves maintaining careful balance and harmony:

- Cohesion Through Materials: Limit texture variety to a few complementary materials—wood, stone, textiles—ensuring each element contributes to overall harmony rather than distraction.
- Consistency in Palette: Keep textures within a consistent, neutral palette. This approach ensures visual coherence, allowing each texture's subtle character to shine without competing for attention.

Light and Texture Interplay

Lighting significantly enhances the visual and tactile richness of textures. Thoughtfully integrated lighting strategies accentuate the subtle depth and warmth of natural materials.

- Directional Lighting: Use focused lighting, such as subtle spotlights or recessed fixtures, to highlight textures, creating beautiful visual interplay of light and shadow.
- Warm Ambient Light: Soft, warm lighting complements natural textures, enhancing their visual appeal and reinforcing an inviting atmosphere.

Maintaining Texture Clarity

Proper care and maintenance of natural textures ensure long-term beauty and warmth:
- Regularly clean and maintain wood, stone, and textile surfaces with appropriate, gentle methods, preserving their natural character.
- Protect delicate surfaces from stains or scratches with sealants or protective treatments, ensuring sustained elegance and comfort.

Final Reflections

Integrating natural textures is central to achieving genuine warmth and comfort in minimalist kitchens. Through careful selection and thoughtful application of wood, stone, textiles, and artisanal accents, your minimalist kitchen transforms into a truly welcoming, comforting, and elegant space. Each interaction becomes tactilely rewarding and visually calming, elevating daily experiences into moments of genuine pleasure and tranquility.

CHAPTER 6
WELCOMING MINIMALIST ENTRIES & HALLWAYS

Designing the Perfect First Impression

The entryway of your home is the very first glimpse guests—and you—receive upon entering. Far more than merely functional, it sets the emotional and aesthetic tone for your entire living space. A minimalist entryway crafted with precision conveys calmness, elegance, and intentional simplicity, inviting warmth while immediately communicating your commitment to refined living.

Creating the perfect first impression involves balancing purposeful design, functionality, and the subtle yet powerful impact of minimalist aesthetics.

Purposeful Simplicity

A minimalist entryway succeeds not by volume but by intention. Every object placed here must serve a clear and purposeful role, whether functional or aesthetic, ensuring visual clarity and immediate tranquility upon entering.

Less is More:
- Limit furnishings to essential, highly functional items—perhaps a simple console, streamlined bench, or sleek coat hooks. Fewer pieces mean more breathing space, allowing visitors to feel instantly at ease.

Thoughtful Furniture Selection:
- Choose furniture with clean, elegant lines that enhance the visual simplicity of your entryway. Opt for materials like natural wood, metal, or glass to reflect subtle sophistication without cluttering the visual field.

Clear Visual Pathways

Entryways should naturally guide visitors into your home. Creating clear visual and physical pathways enhances ease of movement and instantly communicates calm efficiency.

Strategic Furniture Placement:
- Arrange furniture to allow smooth, intuitive flow. Keep paths unobstructed, allowing easy transitions from entryway to adjacent spaces, emphasizing openness and accessibility.

Balanced Proportions:
- Proportional balance is vital. Furniture should neither dominate the space nor appear lost within it. Properly scaled furnishings ensure visual harmony, reinforcing the calm ambiance of minimalist design.

Minimalist Storage Solutions

Entryways naturally accumulate personal belongings, shoes, keys, and outerwear. Integrating discreet storage solutions ensures clutter remains invisible, preserving minimalist clarity.

Hidden Storage:
- Built-in cabinets, concealed drawers, or sleek storage benches store essentials discreetly yet accessibly. These solutions reduce visual clutter, promoting tranquility and enhancing functionality.

Multi-Functional Pieces:
- Choose furniture items that provide dual functionality, such as benches with hidden storage compartments or streamlined wall-mounted shelves serving as decor and practical storage simultaneously.

The Power of Negative Space

In minimalist entryways, negative space is not emptiness—it's purposeful design. Empty areas surrounding furnishings and decor provide visual rest and create a profound sense of calm openness.

Intentional Emptiness:
- Resist the urge to fill every wall or surface. Purposeful emptiness enhances the impact of each carefully selected item, providing visual clarity and emotional calmness upon entering.

Balanced Decorative Elements:
- Decorative objects or art, if included, should be carefully curated, subtly placed, and few in number. A single piece of art, a sculptural object, or a striking vase becomes significantly impactful when surrounded by negative space.

Natural Elements and Lighting

Natural textures, organic elements, and intentional lighting create warmth and elevate the entryway experience, softening minimalism's perceived austerity.

Integrating Nature:
- Incorporate subtle natural textures such as wooden flooring, stone accents, or small plants. Organic materials and greenery immediately convey warmth and a welcoming atmosphere.

Lighting as Invitation:
- Lighting significantly shapes the first impression. Opt for soft, diffused lighting sources—such as wall sconces, ceiling fixtures, or recessed lighting—to gently illuminate the space. Natural daylight, enhanced by minimal window treatments or mirrors, adds brightness and openness.

Subtle Color Choices

Color palettes in minimalist entryways should reflect soothing sophistication. Neutral tones or soft, muted colors create an inviting, calm first impression.

Neutral and Muted Tones:
- Choose shades such as whites, grays, soft earth tones, or subtle pastels to evoke tranquility. These hues enhance visual harmony and support the minimalist aesthetic, inviting visitors with understated elegance.

Consistency in Palette:
- Ensure color consistency between your entryway and adjacent spaces, providing visual continuity and reinforcing overall design coherence.

Reflecting Personal Identity

While minimalist entryways emphasize simplicity, personal touches remain crucial. Thoughtfully chosen items express individuality without overwhelming visual harmony.

Meaningful Objects:
- Include personal items or artwork sparingly and deliberately. A single, significant artwork, photograph, or cherished object can communicate personality without cluttering the aesthetic.

Reflective Mirrors:
- Strategically placed mirrors provide practical function—checking appearance before exiting—and visually expand the space, amplifying openness and brightness.

Creating Lasting Impressions

A well-designed minimalist entryway leaves a lasting impression of intentional simplicity, elegance, and thoughtful hospitality. By meticulously selecting furnishings, strategically managing space, integrating purposeful storage, and subtly incorporating lighting, texture, and color, your entryway becomes a space of genuine welcome—quietly sophisticated, functionally intuitive, and effortlessly elegant.

Every time you or a guest steps into your home, this first impression resonates deeply, setting the tone for the serene and intentional living that defines minimalism at its best.

Hallway Harmony: Elegance and Practicality

Hallways are often overlooked in design, viewed merely as functional spaces connecting rooms. In minimalist design, however, the hallway presents a unique opportunity to express quiet elegance, practicality, and visual coherence. An effectively designed minimalist hallway harmoniously blends aesthetic refinement with intuitive functionality, enhancing daily living through clarity, ease, and thoughtful simplicity.

Creating Flow and Visual Continuity

Hallways in minimalist homes serve as transitional spaces, seamlessly guiding inhabitants from one area to another. Achieving visual harmony means creating a continuous, balanced journey.

Consistency in Design
- Maintain continuity with flooring, colors, and materials from adjacent rooms. A uniform floor material—such as polished concrete, natural wood, or minimalist tiling—helps unify spaces, enhancing the sense of seamless flow.

Proportion and Scale
- Ensure hallway furnishings and decor are proportionate to the space's dimensions. Slim console tables, low benches, or slender wall-mounted shelves fit comfortably without impeding movement, ensuring smooth navigation.

Strategic and Minimalist Furniture Choices

Selecting furniture for minimalist hallways requires thoughtful restraint. Each piece should offer clear functionality without unnecessary visual weight or complexity.

Slim Consoles and Benches
- Choose streamlined, low-profile consoles or benches that provide functional surfaces or seating without cluttering the space. Opt for furniture with clean lines, simple forms, and subtle finishes.

Functional Multi-Use Pieces
- Furniture serving multiple roles is particularly valuable. For instance, benches with built-in storage or sleek wall-mounted shelving units double as decor and practical surfaces, maximizing hallway functionality without visual clutter.

Sophisticated Storage Solutions

Hallways naturally accumulate items—keys, mail, outerwear, or shoes. Sophisticated, discreet storage solutions are crucial in preserving visual harmony and practical functionality.

Hidden or Integrated Storage
- Incorporate hidden compartments, recessed cabinetry, or integrated storage systems designed to blend subtly into walls. These solutions maintain clarity, providing essential storage without sacrificing minimalist aesthetics.

Open Storage with Intention
- If open storage is employed, it must be intentional and aesthetically cohesive. Carefully curated open shelves can elegantly display a select few items, providing practical access and subtle decoration.

Thoughtful Lighting for Clarity and Ambiance

Lighting significantly influences hallway harmony, providing practical visibility and enhancing the visual elegance of minimalist design.

Ambient and Task Lighting
- Combine ambient lighting—such as recessed ceiling fixtures or unobtrusive sconces—with subtle task lighting to illuminate artwork, mirrors, or functional surfaces clearly yet softly.

Strategic Placement
- Position lights thoughtfully along hallway lengths, guiding visual movement. This approach enhances spaciousness, maintains visual clarity, and subtly emphasizes architectural features or decorative elements.

Minimalist Decorative Accents

While minimalism prioritizes simplicity, carefully selected decorative accents add personal warmth and visual interest, enhancing the hallway's welcoming atmosphere.

Limited Artworks
- Choose one or two impactful artworks or photographs placed strategically. A single piece can create a significant impression, emphasizing elegance without overwhelming visual calmness.

Subtle Mirrors and Textural Elements
- Strategically placed mirrors enhance spaciousness and brightness. Additionally, subtle textural accents—such as textured wallpaper, understated ceramics, or woven wall hangings—can introduce visual depth without compromising simplicity.

Integrating Natural Textures for Warmth

Introducing natural textures—wood, stone, or subtle textiles—provides sensory warmth, transforming minimalist hallways from purely functional spaces into inviting passages.

Organic Materials
- Utilize materials such as natural wood flooring or stone accents to infuse subtle warmth. These materials balance visual simplicity with tactile comfort, making hallways welcoming yet understated.

Soft Textiles
- Incorporate restrained textile elements, such as runners or subtle wall hangings, to add softness and comfort underfoot or visually enrich the space without clutter.

Maintaining Practicality and Ease of Use

A minimalist hallway must not only look elegant but also function intuitively in daily life. Practicality ensures the space remains consistently harmonious, clear, and easy to navigate.

Efficient Flow and Accessibility
- Prioritize efficient movement with clear, unobstructed pathways. Ensure functional elements—such as hooks, shelves, or storage—are within easy reach and logically placed.

Daily Maintenance Simplicity
- Select durable, easy-to-clean surfaces and materials. Simplicity in upkeep ensures your hallway retains its elegant clarity effortlessly, maintaining minimalist harmony over time.

Achieving hallway harmony in minimalist design involves balancing aesthetics, functionality, and thoughtful intentionality. By carefully curating furniture, strategically integrating storage, and subtly incorporating textures and lighting, your hallway becomes far more than just a passage—it evolves into a refined space, seamlessly blending elegance and practicality. Each transition through your home becomes a moment of gentle sophistication, reinforcing the tranquility and clarity central to minimalist living.

CHAPTER 7
THE LUXURIOUS MINIMALIST BATHROOM

Achieving Spa-Like Simplicity

Your bathroom is more than a functional necessity—it's a sanctuary, a personal retreat within your home where simplicity and luxury coexist effortlessly. A luxurious minimalist bathroom invites tranquility, evoking the calm, rejuvenating atmosphere typically found only in high-end spas. Achieving spa-like simplicity requires careful attention to detail, thoughtful design, and a commitment to visual and tactile harmony.

Creating a Sense of Calm

Spa-like simplicity is fundamentally about calmness—both visual and emotional. Minimalist design achieves this through restraint, intentionality, and a deliberate reduction of visual clutter.

Visual Clarity:
- Opt for a neutral color palette, emphasizing whites, creams, soft grays, or muted earth tones. A restrained palette reduces visual noise, fostering a serene, calming atmosphere.

Negative Space:
- Incorporate generous negative space, intentionally leaving areas clear and unobstructed. This openness enhances a feeling of spaciousness and tranquility, inviting relaxation and mental clarity.

Thoughtful Layout and Flow

A spa-like minimalist bathroom prioritizes intuitive functionality, seamless movement, and comfort. Strategic layout design ensures effortless usability and peaceful enjoyment.

Zoning for Serenity:
- Clearly delineate zones for bathing, grooming, and storage. Each area should flow naturally into the next, creating intuitive transitions and minimizing visual disruptions.

Focus on Proportions:
- Fixtures and fittings must be proportionate to room size and layout, promoting visual harmony. Properly scaled bathtubs, sinks, showers, and cabinetry ensure balanced visual weight and maximum comfort.

Sleek, Spa-Inspired Fixtures

Choosing bathroom fixtures thoughtfully enhances the spa-like aesthetic, subtly emphasizing elegance and simplicity.

Freestanding or Integrated Tubs:
- A freestanding bathtub instantly conveys luxury, providing a central visual anchor. If space is limited, elegantly integrated soaking tubs or minimalist walk-in showers offer equally calming experiences.

Simple, Streamlined Sinks:
- Opt for sleek basins, either wall-mounted or integrated into minimalist cabinetry. Clean lines, simple shapes, and unobtrusive faucets maintain visual clarity and reinforce tranquility.

Sophisticated Faucets and Hardware:
- Select faucets, handles, and fixtures with minimalist designs—smooth lines, subtle curves, and matte or brushed finishes add sophistication without overwhelming simplicity.

Luxurious Yet Functional Surfaces

In a minimalist bathroom, surfaces play a crucial role, blending practical functionality with spa-like luxury. Choose materials that offer tactile pleasure, aesthetic simplicity, and ease of maintenance.

Natural Stone and Tile:
Stone surfaces such as marble, quartz, limestone, or terrazzo immediately evoke spa-like elegance. Minimalist tiles, either large-format or subtle mosaics, further enhance visual tranquility.

Warm Wood Accents:
Wood introduces warmth, grounding the minimalist aesthetic and providing tactile comfort. Use wood accents sparingly—perhaps cabinetry, shelving, or accessories—to maintain simplicity.

Glass for Transparency:
Transparent or subtly frosted glass shower enclosures or partitions preserve visual openness, enhancing spaciousness and lightness.

Ambient Lighting for Serenity

Lighting significantly shapes your bathroom's spa-like atmosphere. Soft, calming illumination enhances relaxation, reducing stress and promoting mental calmness.

Diffuse Lighting:
- Employ soft, diffused lighting, ideally dimmable, to gently illuminate your bathroom without harsh glare or stark shadows. Indirect lighting behind mirrors, shelves, or within recessed fixtures offers gentle ambiance.

Accent Lighting:
- Subtle accent lighting—such as sconces or pendant lights—highlights architectural features or specific zones, enhancing visual depth and providing intimate illumination.

Minimalist Decor and Spa-Like Accessories

Carefully curated accessories contribute significantly to spa-like simplicity, offering luxurious comfort and practical functionality without visual clutter.

Textural Towels and Robes:
- Invest in high-quality, plush towels and bathrobes, preferably in neutral or muted tones. These textiles contribute tactile richness and immediate luxury.

Natural Elements:
- Incorporate natural accessories—such as wooden bath mats, stone soap dishes, or organic bath brushes—to reinforce spa-like authenticity.

Limited Decor:
- Keep decor minimal and carefully chosen—perhaps a single vase with fresh flowers, a simple tray for essentials, or discreet containers for toiletries.

Ensuring Sensory Pleasure

Spa-like simplicity engages all senses, enhancing relaxation through subtle sensory experiences.

Fragrance and Aromatherapy:
- Incorporate aromatherapy diffusers, scented candles, or natural fragrances to subtly perfume your bathroom, enhancing sensory enjoyment and relaxation.

Sound and Acoustics:
- Consider acoustics carefully—softening surfaces with textiles or incorporating discreet sound systems that offer relaxing music or nature sounds, enhancing tranquility.

Maintaining Spa-Like Simplicity

Sustaining spa-like simplicity involves consistent, mindful maintenance:

- Regularly declutter surfaces and storage areas, keeping only essential items visibly accessible.
- Maintain fixtures, surfaces, and accessories carefully, ensuring long-term visual clarity and tactile comfort.

Achieving spa-like simplicity in a minimalist bathroom transforms ordinary daily routines into luxurious, restorative experiences. Through thoughtful planning, carefully selected fixtures, luxurious materials, calming lighting, and subtle sensory elements, your bathroom evolves into a serene sanctuary—calm, comforting, and effortlessly elegant. Minimalism, in this context, elevates everyday self-care into genuinely indulgent, spa-inspired rituals.

Elevated Materials for Elegant Spaces

In a minimalist bathroom, materials are not merely practical components—they are foundational elements shaping the space's ambiance, aesthetics, and sense of luxury. The selection of materials is pivotal in creating elegant minimalism, providing both tactile pleasure and visual sophistication. Elevated, thoughtfully selected materials transform minimalist bathrooms from merely functional spaces into refined, serene sanctuaries defined by timeless elegance.

The Essence of Material Sophistication

Minimalism emphasizes the beauty inherent in simplicity, making the careful choice of materials crucial. Each selected material should contribute distinctively yet subtly, enriching the space without unnecessary complexity or distraction. Materials in minimalist bathrooms must offer visual harmony, tactile comfort, and enduring quality, seamlessly blending luxury and understated elegance.

Natural Stone: Timeless Elegance

Natural stone surfaces inherently embody refined sophistication, delivering lasting beauty, depth, and tactile pleasure.

Marble:
- Marble is synonymous with luxury. Its subtle veining, muted tones, and gentle reflective quality bring sophistication, serenity, and timeless elegance. Ideal for countertops, floors, walls, or shower enclosures, marble's inherent beauty quietly commands attention.

Quartzite and Granite:
- Quartzite and granite offer durability paired with understated luxury. Their textures and subtle patterns provide visual interest and depth, making them excellent choices for counters and wall cladding.

Travertine and Limestone:
- These stones convey earthy warmth and softness, ideal for floors or walls. Their gentle textures and subdued color palettes enhance tranquility, grounding minimalist spaces elegantly.

Wood: Organic Warmth and Subtle Luxury

Wood is essential for balancing minimalism's sleek simplicity with warmth and comfort, making bathrooms inviting rather than austere.

Teak, Walnut, or Oak:
- Dense, water-resistant woods like teak, walnut, or oak offer durability and visual warmth. Utilize these woods in cabinetry, shelving, or accent pieces, subtly enriching the space's tactile quality.

Wood Accents:
- Wood's warmth can be incorporated minimally yet impactfully through smaller accents—such as wooden bath mats, storage trays, or shelving—providing organic texture and subtle comfort.

Glass: Transparency and Clarity

Glass offers minimalist bathrooms openness, clarity, and visual spaciousness, essential for maintaining elegance and serenity.

Frameless Glass Enclosures:
- Frameless shower doors or enclosures provide unobstructed sightlines, enhancing visual openness and elegance. Clear or subtly frosted glass maintains simplicity and sophistication.

Glass Surfaces and Shelving:
- Glass surfaces—such as minimalist shelving, countertops, or backsplashes—introduce refined subtlety, reflecting light gently and maintaining visual harmony.

Matte and Brushed Metallics: Subtle Luxury

Metallic finishes in minimalist bathrooms introduce gentle sophistication, enhancing visual depth without overwhelming simplicity.

Brushed Metals:
- Brushed finishes in brass, bronze, stainless steel, or matte black lend subtle sophistication. Select faucets, shower fittings, towel rails, and fixtures with minimalist, sleek designs, incorporating gentle metallic accents to elevate visual interest.

Restrained Metallic Usage:
- Use metallics sparingly yet purposefully. Strategic placement of metallic finishes maintains subtle elegance without disrupting minimalist harmony.

Ceramics and Porcelain: Refined Simplicity

High-quality ceramics or porcelain tiles provide elegance, practicality, and consistent visual coherence in minimalist bathrooms.

Large-Format Tiles:
- Large-format ceramic or porcelain tiles reduce visual clutter and seams, creating smooth, expansive surfaces that enhance visual calmness.

Textured or Matte Finishes:
- Matte ceramic or porcelain tiles subtly enrich visual and tactile depth, emphasizing sophistication without excessive reflectivity or glare.

Textiles: Softness and Comfort

Textiles offer essential tactile comfort, reinforcing elegance through softness and sensory indulgence.

Luxurious Towels and Rugs:
- High-quality cotton, linen, or bamboo towels and plush bath rugs add immediate comfort and understated luxury. Neutral tones or gentle textures maintain visual simplicity and serenity.

Window Treatments:
- Soft, minimalist fabric window treatments—such as sheer linen curtains or subtle shades—gently diffuse natural light, enriching the atmosphere with softness and warmth.

Sustainable and Ethical Material Choices

Sustainability aligns inherently with minimalist values—prioritizing quality, longevity, and responsible consumption.

Ethical Sourcing:
- Choose sustainably sourced stone, responsibly harvested woods, recycled glass, or eco-friendly textiles, reflecting environmental consciousness and enhancing the overall elegance of your bathroom.

Durability and Longevity:
- Prioritize materials known for durability and ease of maintenance. Sustainable elegance arises from lasting quality and reduced resource consumption.

Balancing Material Harmony

Effectively combining elevated materials involves intentional restraint and harmony:

- Limit your selection to a few complementary materials—perhaps stone, wood, and glass—ensuring visual coherence.
- Maintain consistent color palettes and textures, subtly enhancing visual depth without unnecessary complexity or clutter.

Elevated materials fundamentally define luxurious minimalist bathrooms. By carefully selecting natural stone, warm woods, transparent glass, refined metallic finishes, elegant ceramics, and comforting textiles, your bathroom transforms into a genuinely sophisticated sanctuary. Each chosen material subtly reinforces elegance, tranquility, and sensory comfort, providing both practical functionality and luxurious indulgence. In minimalist bathrooms, thoughtful material selection elevates simplicity into refined luxury—making everyday rituals deeply comforting, effortlessly sophisticated, and endlessly satisfying.

Intelligent, Hidden Storage Solutions

Minimalist bathrooms derive their calm elegance from visual clarity, achieved through carefully controlled simplicity. Intelligent storage solutions are therefore essential—ensuring necessities remain discreetly hidden yet easily accessible. Integrating hidden storage seamlessly into your bathroom maintains its spa-like serenity and luxurious minimalism, preserving visual tranquility without sacrificing practical functionality.

The Importance of Hidden Storage in Minimalist Bathrooms

Hidden storage is more than a practical necessity; it is an aesthetic cornerstone. It allows surfaces to remain uncluttered, promoting visual calmness and enabling your bathroom to feel spacious, elegant, and inviting.

Reducing Visual Clutter:
- Hidden storage eliminates visual distractions, supporting the sense of tranquility central to minimalist design.

Enhancing Functionality:
- Efficient storage ensures items remain organized, easily accessible, and intuitively arranged, enhancing everyday usability.

Integrated Cabinetry and Concealed Compartments

Built-in cabinetry is a fundamental storage solution for minimalist bathrooms, seamlessly blending into the architecture while providing discreet storage.

Flush Cabinetry:
- Cabinets designed to be flush with walls or mirror surfaces create a smooth visual plane. Opt for cabinets with hidden or minimal handles, promoting seamless integration and understated elegance.

Recessed Shelving and Niches:
- Recessed storage niches, particularly in shower areas, provide subtle spaces for essential toiletries without intruding visually. These niches maintain seamless wall surfaces, eliminating unnecessary protrusions or shelves.

Vanity Storage: Discreet and Efficient

The vanity is a primary storage opportunity in minimalist bathrooms. Efficiently designed vanity units discreetly hide daily essentials, maintaining uncluttered surfaces.

Integrated Drawer Systems:
- Deep, streamlined drawers with internal organizers maximize usability and reduce clutter. Concealed internal compartments store toiletries, cosmetics, and grooming essentials neatly out of sight.

Floating Vanities:
- Floating vanity units enhance visual spaciousness, providing discreet storage while reinforcing minimalist elegance. Open floor space beneath the vanity supports visual openness and easy cleaning.

Mirror Cabinets and Hidden Storage Behind Mirrors

Mirrors offer versatile storage potential, discreetly hiding storage behind reflective surfaces to preserve visual simplicity.

Mirrored Cabinets:
- Integrated mirrored cabinets subtly hide toiletries and bathroom necessities, combining essential functionality and elegant aesthetics. Cabinet doors that seamlessly blend into walls ensure uninterrupted visual calmness.

Sliding Mirror Panels:
- Sliding mirror panels or pivoting mirrors conceal hidden shelving or recessed storage, providing practical accessibility without visual clutter.

Concealed Storage Fixtures

Integrating storage into bathroom fixtures—such as showers, bathtubs, and seating—provides intelligent, unexpected solutions that blend seamlessly with minimalist aesthetics.

Hidden Shower Storage:
- Wall-integrated shelving or recessed niches within showers discreetly house shampoos, soaps, and grooming essentials, reducing visual clutter and enhancing practicality.

Bathtub and Bench Storage:
- Incorporate hidden compartments beneath seating benches or within freestanding bathtub surrounds. Such storage discreetly holds towels, bath essentials, or cleaning products, maintaining visual serenity.

Slimline Storage for Limited Spaces

In smaller bathrooms, intelligent slimline storage solutions are crucial. Vertical storage, narrow shelving units, and subtle wall-mounted units maximize usability without overwhelming limited spaces.

Vertical Cabinets and Towers:
- Narrow, tall cabinets or vertical storage towers maximize vertical space, discreetly housing essentials in a compact footprint.

Wall-Mounted Units:
- Sleek, wall-mounted storage units provide discreet practicality, offering essential storage without occupying valuable floor space.

Pull-Out and Slide-Out Storage

Pull-out or slide-out storage solutions ensure efficient space utilization, providing practical access to hidden items without visual disruption.

Slide-Out Trays and Drawers:
- Narrow slide-out trays or drawers, integrated within cabinetry or behind panels, discreetly store toiletries, cleaning products, or grooming accessories.

Concealed Laundry Baskets:
- Slide-out laundry baskets or hidden hampers neatly integrate dirty linens storage, significantly reducing visual clutter and maintaining a tidy, organized bathroom.

Material and Finish Integration

Materials and finishes for hidden storage should maintain visual coherence with overall bathroom aesthetics, seamlessly blending into the design.

Matching Finishes:
- Select cabinetry, shelving, and storage elements matching walls or fixtures, reinforcing visual continuity and subtle elegance.

Minimal Hardware:
- Use discreet or invisible hardware for cabinetry and storage compartments, ensuring uninterrupted visual clarity and minimalist sophistication.

Sustainable and Durable Storage Solutions

Sustainability and durability remain essential considerations, enhancing minimalist bathroom longevity and eco-friendliness.

Sustainable Materials:
- Choose storage materials responsibly sourced and sustainably produced, enhancing both practicality and ethical integrity.

Durable Finishes and Materials:
- Select storage solutions crafted from robust, moisture-resistant materials and finishes, ensuring durability and long-term practicality.

Maintenance and Organization

Effective hidden storage necessitates ongoing maintenance and thoughtful organization:

- Regularly declutter hidden storage areas, ensuring optimal usability.
- Employ internal organizers to maintain orderly, accessible storage systems.

CHAPTER 8
THE MINIMALIST HOME OFFICE

Productivity Through Elegant Simplicity

In an increasingly busy world, your home office must serve as a sanctuary for productivity, clarity, and creative thought. A minimalist home office achieves precisely this—pairing intentional simplicity with elegant design to enhance efficiency, reduce stress, and inspire deeper focus. By thoughtfully removing distractions and carefully curating your workspace, you empower yourself to achieve more, think clearly, and find genuine joy in everyday work.

The Power of Purposeful Design

A productive minimalist home office begins with purpose-driven design. Every choice, from furniture to layout, should intentionally support your workflow, enhancing both efficiency and visual serenity.

Clear Functional Zones:
- Clearly define zones for tasks such as computer work, writing, storage, or meetings. These designated areas streamline workflow, reducing wasted movement and mental distractions.

Ergonomic Simplicity:
- Ergonomics are crucial—furniture must support your body comfortably. Choose chairs, desks, and accessories ergonomically designed to enhance comfort, posture, and sustained productivity, without unnecessary complexity.

Eliminating Visual and Mental Clutter

Minimalist productivity depends significantly on maintaining visual and mental clarity. Carefully manage and minimize clutter to promote focus, calmness, and efficiency.

Streamlined Work Surfaces:
- Maintain clear, uncluttered surfaces, ensuring only essential items remain visible. Regularly clear unnecessary paperwork, gadgets, or decorative items, keeping visual distractions minimal.

Effective Storage Solutions:
- Implement discreet, integrated storage solutions such as concealed drawers, built-in cabinetry, or minimalist shelving systems. Efficient storage ensures necessary items remain organized yet discreet, reinforcing productivity through clarity.

Selecting Elegant, Functional Furniture

Furniture choices significantly influence both productivity and aesthetics. Each piece of furniture should provide essential functionality without overwhelming visual simplicity.

Minimalist Desks:
- Choose sleek desks with simple lines, ample workspace, and discreet storage capabilities. Consider built-in cable management solutions to reduce visual clutter and enhance functionality.

Supportive, Stylish Seating:
- Opt for minimalist office chairs designed ergonomically, providing sustained comfort without excessive ornamentation. Chairs featuring clean lines and elegant materials enhance both productivity and visual sophistication.

Mindful Tech Integration

Technology significantly shapes productivity. Minimalist home offices carefully integrate technology—ensuring essential devices are accessible yet unobtrusive.

Concealed Cable Management:
- Utilize discreet cable management systems—hidden channels, integrated power strips, or wireless charging pads—to reduce visual and physical clutter.

Streamlined Devices:
- Choose sleek, minimalist tech accessories and devices. Prioritize wireless keyboards, slimline monitors, or elegant docking stations that blend seamlessly with your minimalist aesthetic.

Purposeful Lighting for Enhanced Focus

Lighting profoundly influences productivity, comfort, and overall workspace ambiance. Intentional lighting design enhances visual clarity, reduces eye strain, and promotes sustained productivity.

Layered Lighting:
- Combine ambient lighting—such as ceiling-mounted fixtures or diffused lamps—with focused task lighting. Adjustable desk lamps or strategically positioned wall sconces enhance clarity for reading, writing, or computer work.

Natural Daylight Maximization:
- Maximize natural daylight, which boosts mood, enhances energy levels, and reduces eye strain. Minimalist window treatments ensure maximum daylight exposure while maintaining visual simplicity.

Neutral and Calming Color Palettes

Color significantly influences productivity, mood, and visual clarity. Select palettes that enhance concentration, reduce visual fatigue, and contribute to overall workspace tranquility.

Calming Neutral Tones:
- Opt for calming, neutral shades—soft whites, grays, muted earth tones, or gentle pastels—reinforcing tranquility and sustained focus.

Consistent and Cohesive:
- Maintain consistency in color choices across furniture, walls, and decor, enhancing visual harmony and further reducing distractions.

Incorporating Minimalist Decor Thoughtfully

Minimalism doesn't exclude decor—rather, it emphasizes careful selection and thoughtful placement. Strategically incorporate decor to inspire creativity, personalize your space, and maintain visual simplicity.

Curated Artwork and Objects:
- Select one or two pieces of artwork or personal objects that genuinely inspire or motivate. Strategically place these items to enhance visual interest without disrupting productivity.

Personal yet Minimal:
- Display personal items minimally and intentionally—perhaps a cherished photograph, a meaningful book, or a simple plant. Each item should enrich your workspace without cluttering it.

Regular Maintenance for Lasting Clarity

Sustaining productivity in your minimalist office involves ongoing mindful maintenance:

- Regularly declutter, keeping your workspace organized, functional, and visually clear.
- Consistently evaluate your workspace, removing unnecessary items and refining your environment to maintain sustained productivity and mental clarity.

Achieving productivity through elegant simplicity in a minimalist home office transforms how you experience daily work. Through thoughtful planning, ergonomic furniture choices, mindful technology integration, strategic lighting, and carefully curated decor, your workspace becomes more than functional—it evolves into a serene, productive sanctuary. Embracing minimalist principles elevates your work experience, empowering clarity, sustained focus, and genuine enjoyment in every task.

Essential Furnishings and Tech Integration

In a minimalist home office, furnishings and technology aren't just practical necessities—they represent thoughtful choices that define your workspace's functionality, aesthetics, and productivity. Essential furnishings must embody both simplicity and elegance, while tech integration should enhance functionality without introducing visual clutter. By carefully selecting and integrating these elements, your minimalist workspace achieves an optimal balance of form and function, supporting productivity and creative inspiration seamlessly.

The Core of Minimalist Furnishings

Essential furnishings in minimalist home offices embody clarity, simplicity, and precise functionality. Each item should perform its role perfectly, contributing subtly yet distinctly to overall workspace harmony.

Minimalist Desks:
- Your desk serves as the workspace's centerpiece. Opt for sleek designs characterized by clean, geometric lines and minimal detailing. Choose desks with ample workspace, discreet drawers, or integrated cable management solutions. Materials such as solid wood, tempered glass, or matte-finished metals enhance tactile comfort and visual elegance.

Streamlined Seating:
- The right office chair is essential for sustained productivity and physical comfort. Select ergonomically designed seating featuring elegant simplicity, adjustable ergonomics, supportive cushioning, and subtle aesthetics. Chairs upholstered in neutral or muted tones harmonize effortlessly with your minimalist workspace.

Intuitive Storage Solutions

Effective storage furnishings significantly impact workspace clarity, maintaining an organized environment that enhances productivity without visual disruption.

Integrated Cabinets and Drawers:
- Choose cabinetry or drawer units designed to integrate seamlessly with your workspace. Sleek built-in cabinets, low-profile filing drawers, or subtle storage units keep essential items discreetly organized, maintaining visual tranquility.

Open Shelving (Selectively Used):
- Open shelving, if carefully curated, offers practical functionality and subtle visual interest. Limit displayed items to essentials or meaningful objects, ensuring shelves remain uncluttered and visually pleasing.

Mindful Tech Integration

Integrating technology into a minimalist workspace demands careful selection and strategic placement. Each technological element should enhance productivity without compromising visual harmony or creating unnecessary distractions.

Sleek Monitors and Devices:
- Select slimline monitors, sleek laptops, or compact desktop units with elegant, minimalist designs. Opt for matte finishes, minimal bezels, and subtle colors that blend discreetly into your workspace.

Wireless and Streamlined Accessories:
- Embrace wireless solutions such as Bluetooth keyboards, mice, speakers, or charging stations, reducing cable clutter and preserving visual clarity.

Effective Cable Management

Discreet cable management is crucial to maintaining visual and practical workspace clarity. Efficient solutions hide or minimize cables, enhancing aesthetics and reducing distractions.

Integrated Cable Channels:
- Employ built-in cable management channels or desk-integrated systems to conceal wiring. Consider desks specifically designed with hidden compartments or cable trays.

Wireless and Concealed Outlets:
- Position electrical outlets strategically to remain hidden or minimally visible. Integrated power strips, concealed wall outlets, or wireless charging pads significantly reduce visible clutter.

Lighting Fixtures for Productivity and Elegance

Effective minimalist office lighting fixtures provide practical visibility, reduce eye strain, and subtly enhance aesthetic appeal.

Adjustable Task Lighting:
- Adjustable, minimalist desk lamps offer targeted illumination essential for specific tasks such as reading or writing, enhancing visual comfort and sustained productivity.

Subtle Ambient Lighting:
- Soft ambient lighting—such as minimalist ceiling fixtures, wall sconces, or discreetly recessed lights—provides gentle overall illumination, promoting visual harmony and reducing workspace glare.

Comfort-Enhancing Textiles

Even minimalist workspaces benefit from tactile comfort—carefully selected textiles contribute significantly to overall workspace satisfaction and productivity.

Understated Rugs:
- A subtle, high-quality rug beneath your desk or seating area enhances tactile comfort and acoustic warmth. Select neutral colors or gentle patterns to maintain visual simplicity.

Minimalist Window Treatments:
- Soft, sheer curtains or simple roller blinds diffuse daylight gently, maintaining optimal workspace illumination without unnecessary visual complexity.

Materials and Finishes: Consistency and Quality

Materials and finishes for essential furnishings and tech items should reinforce workspace harmony, offering subtle elegance and durable practicality.

Consistent Material Choices:
- Choose complementary materials—such as wood, metal, glass, or matte finishes—ensuring visual coherence and subtle sophistication throughout the workspace.

Quality and Durability:
- Prioritize furnishings and technology renowned for durability and timeless design. High-quality materials ensure lasting functionality and consistent aesthetic pleasure.

Sustainable and Ethical Considerations

Mindful minimalism inherently aligns with sustainability and ethical considerations:

Eco-Friendly Furnishings:
- Choose sustainably sourced or responsibly manufactured furnishings, reflecting ecological consciousness and ethical integrity.

Energy-Efficient Technology:
- Select energy-efficient devices and appliances, ensuring your minimalist workspace remains environmentally responsible.

Maintaining an Optimal Workspace

Regular maintenance ensures sustained productivity and continued visual clarity in your minimalist workspace:

- Regularly declutter and organize storage and desk spaces, removing unnecessary items to maintain visual simplicity.
- Periodically reassess technology integration, updating or replacing devices to ensure continued functionality and aesthetic coherence.

Essential furnishings and mindful tech integration profoundly shape the minimalist home office experience. By carefully selecting ergonomic, elegant furnishings, implementing intelligent storage solutions, and discreetly integrating advanced technology, your workspace becomes more than just functional—it evolves into a calming, productive sanctuary. This intentional approach to design significantly enhances daily productivity, creativity, and overall well-being, elevating every task performed within your minimalist home office into an effortlessly enjoyable experience.

Greenery and Personal Touches Without Clutter

Introducing greenery and personal elements into a minimalist home office enriches the space with warmth, personality, and visual interest, without detracting from the principles of simplicity and clarity. Plants and carefully selected personal touches provide emotional comfort, inspiration, and a sense of calm, turning your workspace into a personalized sanctuary that remains refined, uncluttered, and deeply inviting.

The Subtle Power of Greenery

Plants breathe life and freshness into minimalist spaces, offering visual serenity, improved air quality, and subtle emotional well-being. Introducing greenery thoughtfully enriches your workspace aesthetically and emotionally without compromising minimalist elegance.

Air-Purifying Plants:
- Select plants known for their air-purifying properties—such as snake plants, peace lilies, pothos, or aloe vera—enhancing workspace air quality and personal well-being.

Minimalist Plant Displays:
- Opt for sleek, minimalist planters made of materials like matte ceramics, concrete, or natural stone. Limit plant placements to one or two strategic locations—such as a desk corner or shelving—to maintain visual simplicity and harmony.

Choosing the Right Plants

Selecting appropriate plants ensures visual balance, minimal upkeep, and effective aesthetic enhancement in your minimalist workspace.

Low-Maintenance Varieties:
- Prioritize resilient, low-maintenance plants requiring minimal watering and care, such as succulents, ZZ plants, or rubber plants. This practicality ensures plants remain visually appealing without adding workload or clutter.

Balanced Plant Sizes:
- Choose plants proportionate to your workspace—larger statement plants for spacious offices, smaller desktop plants for compact spaces. Properly sized plants reinforce visual harmony, maintaining minimalist clarity.

Strategic Greenery Placement

Strategic placement of plants significantly impacts their visual effectiveness and workspace tranquility.

Desktop and Shelving:
- Small, unobtrusive plants placed on desks or shelves introduce gentle greenery, enhancing visual comfort without overcrowding.

Floor Standing Plants:
- For larger home offices, minimalist floor-standing plants—such as fiddle-leaf figs or rubber trees—act as elegant focal points, grounding the workspace without dominating visually.

Introducing Personal Touches Mindfully

Minimalism doesn't mean eliminating personality—it emphasizes mindful curation. Thoughtfully selected personal touches reflect your individuality, inspire productivity, and provide emotional comfort without cluttering your workspace.

Curated Artwork:
- Select one or two impactful art pieces or framed prints that resonate personally or creatively inspire you. Art should blend harmoniously with the workspace's overall aesthetic, adding subtle visual depth without overwhelming simplicity.

Meaningful Objects:
- Include a small number of cherished personal items, such as a significant photograph, minimalist sculpture, or sentimental object. Each piece should hold emotional significance, reinforcing workspace warmth without clutter.

Minimalist Displays and Groupings

Displaying greenery and personal items minimally and intentionally ensures visual harmony, preventing clutter and distractions.

Small Groupings:
- If grouping plants or personal objects, keep collections limited to three items or fewer. Odd-numbered groupings appear naturally balanced, enhancing visual appeal while maintaining simplicity.

Negative Space as Balance:
- Surround plants and personal items with intentional negative space, enhancing their visual impact. Negative space reinforces tranquility, providing essential visual breathing room.

Functional Personal Items

Personal items serving dual purposes—both functional and decorative—align perfectly with minimalist principles:

Stylish Notebooks or Desk Accessories:
- Choose visually appealing, minimalist notebooks, organizers, or accessories, providing practical functionality while subtly enriching workspace aesthetics.

Personalized Desk Mats or Mouse Pads:
- Elegant desk mats or minimalist mouse pads offer functional usability while subtly incorporating personal style or preferred colors.

Subtle Color and Texture Integration

Greenery and personal touches introduce subtle variations in color and texture, enriching visual and tactile workspace experiences without overwhelming visual harmony.

Gentle Color Accents:
- Select plants and decor in muted, natural shades—soft greens, neutral ceramics, or subtle metallic accents—complementing your workspace's existing color palette.

Textural Enrichment:
- Introduce gentle textural contrasts through plants, ceramics, or fabrics, subtly enhancing tactile and visual depth without compromising minimalist simplicity.

Sustaining Minimalist Clarity

Maintaining clarity and simplicity involves continuous mindful management of greenery and personal items:

Regular Pruning and Care:
- Regularly maintain plants—pruning, watering, and caring appropriately—to ensure sustained visual appeal and minimal upkeep.

Consistent Reassessment:
- Periodically evaluate your personal touches, removing or updating items as needed. Ensure displayed items continually inspire, resonate personally, and support sustained productivity.

CHAPTER 9
MINIMALISM OUTDOORS

Refined Outdoor Living Spaces

Extending minimalist principles to your outdoor spaces creates an elegant, tranquil environment that seamlessly bridges interior simplicity with the natural world. Refined outdoor living spaces embody the essence of minimalism—emphasizing clarity, intentionality, and subtle sophistication. When thoughtfully designed, your minimalist outdoor space becomes a tranquil retreat, providing both aesthetic pleasure and practical functionality, inviting restful contemplation and enhancing everyday well-being.

Embracing Simplicity and Clarity

Minimalist outdoor living prioritizes visual clarity and intentionality, ensuring every element contributes distinctly and harmoniously to the overall design.

Clear Layout and Functionality:
- Clearly define functional zones—dining areas, lounge spaces, quiet retreats—with strategic layouts. Avoid unnecessary complexity or visual clutter, allowing each space to remain visually open and accessible.

Focused Elements:
- Limit furnishings and decor to essential, high-quality items. A select few well-chosen pieces—such as a streamlined lounge chair, a minimalist dining set, or subtle garden accents—maintain visual clarity and enhance sophisticated simplicity.

Seamless Transitions from Indoors to Outdoors

Minimalist outdoor living spaces harmoniously extend your home's interior aesthetics outward, creating visual and emotional continuity.

Material and Color Consistency:
- Maintain consistency in flooring materials, colors, or textures, seamlessly blending interior and exterior spaces. Uniform materials, such as natural stone, concrete, or decking, promote visual harmony and effortless transitions.

Visual Flow:
- Align furniture placement, pathways, and landscaping elements strategically to reinforce visual and physical transitions, emphasizing an intuitive flow from indoors to outdoors.

Natural Materials and Textures

Incorporating natural materials provides warmth, authenticity, and elegant simplicity, enhancing sensory richness and visual sophistication.

Stone and Concrete:
- Natural stone, polished concrete, or subtle gravel pathways offer visual tranquility and tactile sophistication, reinforcing minimalism's quiet elegance.

Wooden Elements:
- Incorporate wooden decking, benches, or pergolas crafted from sustainably sourced woods like teak, cedar, or ipe. Wood introduces organic warmth, complementing minimalist clarity with subtle depth and comfort.

Minimalist Landscaping Elements:
- Integrate minimal landscaping elements, such as geometric stone pathways, simple water features, or restrained planting areas, to maintain visual harmony and subtle natural interest.

Functional and Uncluttered Furnishings

Outdoor furnishings in minimalist spaces must combine elegance, practicality, and restrained simplicity.

Streamlined Seating and Tables:
- Choose furniture with clean lines, simple silhouettes, and minimalist detailing. Opt for pieces that reflect intentional craftsmanship, emphasizing form, function, and visual serenity.

Multifunctional and Modular Options:
- Consider modular seating or multi-purpose furnishings that adapt easily to different outdoor activities or gatherings, reinforcing both practicality and minimalist versatility.

Intentional Lighting and Ambience

Effective lighting significantly shapes your outdoor space's ambiance, enhancing evening usability and reinforcing minimalist tranquility.

Ambient and Accent Lighting:
- Incorporate soft ambient lighting—such as discreet recessed fixtures or minimalist wall sconces—combined with subtle accent lighting to illuminate focal points, pathways, or specific landscaping elements.

Strategic Light Placement:
- Position lighting thoughtfully, subtly enhancing architectural or natural features without creating visual clutter or unnecessary brightness.

Carefully Curated Greenery

Minimalist outdoor spaces thoughtfully incorporate greenery, balancing natural beauty and visual simplicity.

Limited Plant Varieties:
- Select a few complementary plant types or trees, reinforcing visual coherence and restrained elegance. Minimalist landscaping emphasizes simplicity, opting for fewer varieties arranged intentionally.

Geometric Plant Arrangements:
- Employ geometric arrangements or clean-lined planters, subtly emphasizing symmetry or deliberate asymmetry to enhance visual clarity and sophisticated minimalism.

Subtle Decorative Elements

Outdoor decor, minimally integrated, enhances visual interest without overwhelming simplicity.

Simple Water Features or Sculptures:
- Integrate discreet water features, minimalist sculptures, or subtle ceramic accents, enhancing sensory richness and gentle visual interest without clutter.

Minimalist Outdoor Textiles:
- Include subtle, weather-resistant textiles—such as neutral outdoor cushions or rugs—providing tactile comfort and elegant softness without disrupting visual harmony.

Sustainable and Eco-Friendly Choices

Sustainability remains integral to minimalist outdoor living, reflecting environmental responsibility and enhancing long-term enjoyment.

Eco-Friendly Furnishings:
- Select outdoor furniture crafted from sustainable materials or recycled components, reflecting responsible minimalism and ethical consciousness.

Natural Landscaping and Water Conservation:
- Incorporate drought-resistant plants, permeable paving, or rainwater harvesting solutions, supporting environmental sustainability while reinforcing minimalist practicality.

Regular Maintenance for Lasting Elegance

Maintaining minimalist outdoor elegance involves consistent care and mindful upkeep:

- Regularly declutter outdoor spaces, removing unnecessary items or foliage to preserve visual clarity.
- Maintain furniture, lighting, and landscaping carefully, ensuring lasting aesthetic integrity and enduring enjoyment.

Refined outdoor living spaces extend minimalist elegance beyond interior boundaries, creating tranquil retreats of clarity, intentionality, and sophisticated simplicity. Thoughtful layouts, seamless indoor-outdoor transitions, carefully selected materials, purposeful furnishings, and restrained decor ensure your minimalist outdoor space remains consistently inviting, peaceful, and elegant. Minimalism outdoors transforms everyday relaxation or socializing into deeply satisfying experiences—calming, luxurious, and harmoniously integrated with your overall lifestyle.

Selecting Exceptional Outdoor Furniture

In minimalist outdoor spaces, each furniture piece is more than merely functional—it defines the essence of your environment, shaping its elegance, comfort, and practical usability. Selecting exceptional outdoor furniture demands thoughtful consideration, prioritizing quality, simplicity, and durability. When carefully curated, your minimalist outdoor furniture elevates every moment spent outdoors, blending effortlessly into the landscape and enhancing your experience of refined, intentional living.

Quality Craftsmanship and Durability

Outdoor furniture in minimalist settings must withstand both visual scrutiny and environmental conditions. Exceptional pieces offer impeccable craftsmanship, longevity, and elegant simplicity.

Weather-Resistant Materials:
- Select furniture crafted from durable, weather-resistant materials like teak, stainless steel, powder-coated aluminum, or all-weather fabrics. These materials age gracefully, maintaining visual integrity and functionality season after season.

Meticulous Craftsmanship:
- Prioritize furniture with refined detailing, precise joinery, and smooth finishes, reflecting intentionality and sophisticated elegance essential to minimalist aesthetics.

Sleek, Streamlined Silhouettes

Minimalist outdoor furniture is defined by clean lines, streamlined forms, and subtle proportions, offering visual tranquility without unnecessary ornamentation.

Simple Geometric Shapes:
- Opt for furniture characterized by straightforward geometric shapes—square, rectangular, or gently rounded edges—enhancing visual simplicity and harmony.

Low-Profile and Open Designs:
- Low-profile seating or tables with open, airy structures promote visual openness and spatial clarity, crucial for minimalist outdoor elegance.

Comfort Without Clutter

Minimalist outdoor furniture emphasizes practical comfort as strongly as visual clarity. Each furniture piece must be ergonomically designed, offering inviting usability without sacrificing visual harmony.

Ergonomic Seating:
- Choose chairs, loungers, and sofas that provide supportive comfort through ergonomically contoured designs. Select cushions with subtle thicknesses, neutral tones, and weather-resistant fabrics, enhancing comfort without visual bulkiness.

Functional Tables and Surfaces:
- Tables should provide practical functionality with clean, uncluttered surfaces—opt for sleek dining tables, minimalist coffee tables, or subtle side tables that integrate seamlessly within the space.

Flexible and Modular Furnishing Options

Flexibility and adaptability enhance minimalist outdoor spaces, allowing effortless adjustment for varied uses or gatherings.

Modular Furniture:
- Modular outdoor seating or furniture systems adapt easily to different arrangements or spatial configurations, supporting minimalist flexibility and sustained usability.

Multi-Purpose Furnishings:
- Multi-functional outdoor furniture—such as benches with hidden storage or tables that double as seating—reinforce practical versatility without visual clutter.

Integrating Furniture with Natural Surroundings

Furniture in minimalist outdoor spaces should harmonize seamlessly with natural surroundings, subtly enhancing the outdoor environment rather than dominating it.

Natural Finishes and Colors:
- Choose furnishings in muted or natural color tones—soft grays, warm woods, subtle metallics, or earthy neutrals—blending unobtrusively into your landscape.

Balanced Placement:
- Arrange furniture strategically to complement natural views, landscaping elements, or architectural features, creating visual balance and intuitive spatial flow.

Exceptional Outdoor Textiles

Carefully selected outdoor textiles significantly enhance comfort, visual interest, and tactile richness, subtly enriching minimalist outdoor spaces.

Neutral Outdoor Fabrics:
- Opt for high-quality outdoor cushions, pillows, or upholstered furnishings in neutral, muted colors. Weather-resistant fabrics such as Sunbrella or solution-dyed acrylic ensure lasting comfort, visual clarity, and practical durability.

Subtle Textural Interest:
- Introduce subtle textile variations—softly woven textures, gentle patterns, or matte finishes—adding quiet visual interest without compromising minimalist simplicity.

Mindful Use of Accent Pieces

Minimalist outdoor spaces benefit from thoughtfully placed accent furniture, enhancing visual interest and practical functionality without clutter.

Statement Chairs or Loungers:
- Introduce one or two statement seating pieces—such as a sculptural lounge chair or minimalist daybed—that subtly anchor visual interest and comfort.

Minimalist Outdoor Accessories:
- Include carefully selected accessories, such as sleek side tables, elegant serving carts, or discreet ottomans, providing practical usability and gentle visual interest.

Sustainable and Ethical Choices

Sustainability remains integral to minimalist values, influencing furniture choices that reflect ecological consciousness and ethical responsibility.

Eco-Friendly Materials:
- Select outdoor furniture crafted from sustainable, recycled, or environmentally responsible materials, reinforcing minimalist practicality and ecological commitment.

Ethically Produced Furnishings:
- Choose furniture from ethical, responsible manufacturers committed to fair labor practices and sustainable production processes.

Maintenance and Care for Longevity

Minimalist outdoor furniture requires consistent care to preserve aesthetic integrity and practical functionality over time:

- Regularly clean and maintain furniture according to recommended guidelines, ensuring continued visual elegance and durability.
- Protect furnishings during extreme weather conditions or off-season periods, ensuring sustained beauty and usability.

Biophilic Design: Connecting Indoors with Nature

Biophilic design—the intentional integration of nature into living spaces—harmonizes perfectly with minimalist principles, emphasizing the profound relationship between human well-being and the natural environment. When thoughtfully applied, biophilic design transforms minimalist spaces into nurturing, restorative environments. By connecting indoors and outdoors seamlessly, it enhances visual tranquility, emotional comfort, and overall quality of life, promoting deeper relaxation and sustained well-being.

Understanding Biophilic Design

Biophilic design focuses on fostering a meaningful, tangible connection between people and nature. Beyond merely aesthetic, it positively influences emotional health, reducing stress and enhancing creativity and productivity.

Natural Light:
- Maximizing natural daylight creates an uplifting, energizing atmosphere, directly supporting mood, concentration, and overall well-being.

Organic Forms and Patterns:
- Incorporating subtle, nature-inspired forms or patterns introduces visual harmony, reinforcing natural connections and emotional comfort.

Bringing Nature Indoors

Seamlessly integrating natural elements indoors reinforces biophilic connections, subtly enriching minimalist spaces without visual complexity.

Plants and Greenery:
- Strategically place indoor plants—such as fiddle-leaf figs, monstera, or succulents—to create visual and emotional tranquility. Select planters with minimalist designs and neutral tones, enhancing aesthetic coherence.

Natural Materials:
- Incorporate wood, stone, bamboo, or natural fibers into interiors, providing tactile comfort, visual warmth, and subtle organic textures.

Enhancing Views and Sightlines

Carefully framing natural views or creating intentional sightlines profoundly strengthens indoor-outdoor connections, enhancing biophilic effectiveness.

Large Windows and Glass Doors:
- Incorporate expansive windows or sliding glass doors, allowing seamless visual access to gardens, landscapes, or natural surroundings, inviting nature visually into interiors.

Framed Natural Features:
- Strategically position windows or architectural features to frame natural focal points—trees, water features, or landscapes—subtly enhancing indoor spaces with organic visuals.

Blurring Indoor-Outdoor Boundaries

Effective biophilic design subtly blurs indoor-outdoor boundaries, creating harmonious, integrated environments.

Consistent Material Choices:
- Employ consistent materials and colors across indoor and outdoor areas, fostering visual continuity and seamless spatial transitions.

Transitional Spaces:
- Design transitional spaces—such as covered terraces, verandas, or garden rooms—providing comfortable, sheltered environments that blend indoor comfort with outdoor openness.

Natural Light Optimization

Maximizing natural daylight is fundamental to biophilic minimalist design, enhancing emotional well-being and visual simplicity.

Minimal Window Treatments:
- Utilize sheer, minimalist curtains or simple blinds, diffusing daylight softly while maintaining visual clarity and openness.

Skylights and Clerestory Windows:
- Integrate skylights or clerestory windows to introduce overhead daylight, significantly enhancing visual brightness, spaciousness, and emotional comfort.

Water Elements for Serenity

Incorporating water features subtly reinforces biophilic connections, promoting tranquility and sensory richness without clutter.

Minimalist Indoor Fountains or Reflective Pools:
- Consider discreet indoor water features—such as minimalist wall fountains or reflective pools—providing gentle auditory and visual serenity, reinforcing emotional calmness.

Outdoor Water Integration:
- Integrate understated outdoor water elements—such as reflecting pools, minimalist fountains, or shallow water channels—enhancing outdoor tranquility and visual beauty.

Organic Shapes and Textures

Introducing subtle organic shapes or natural textures provides visual softness, emotional comfort, and refined elegance.

Rounded Furniture and Fixtures:
- Incorporate furniture or architectural elements with gentle curves or rounded forms, subtly echoing natural organic shapes and providing visual harmony.

Textural Natural Fabrics:
- Select natural textiles—linen, wool, or cotton—with gentle textures, enriching tactile comfort and subtle visual interest without complexity.

Eco-Friendly and Sustainable Design Choices

Sustainability inherently aligns with biophilic minimalist design, reflecting environmental consciousness and ethical responsibility.

Sustainable Materials:
- Choose sustainably harvested woods, natural fibers, recycled materials, or low-impact finishes, ensuring environmental responsibility and aesthetic harmony.

Energy Efficiency and Eco-Friendly Practices:
- Integrate energy-efficient systems—natural ventilation, passive heating, solar shading—enhancing comfort while promoting ecological responsibility.

Maintenance and Preservation

Maintaining biophilic connections involves ongoing mindful care and intentional upkeep:

- Regularly maintain greenery, water features, and natural materials to preserve aesthetic integrity and biophilic effectiveness.
- Consistently manage indoor-outdoor connections, ensuring continued visual harmony and spatial coherence.

GALLERY OF INSPIRATION

JAPANDI

SL

STUDIOLUX

BECOME ICONIC—MAKE YOUR STYLE VIRAL WITH US

You've selected "Less & Serene", a statement addition to your beautiful home.

Now it's your moment in the spotlight! Create a captivating video or sophisticated photograph featuring "Less & Serene" and share your creation on Instagram, TikTok, or Facebook using the hashtag #StudioLux. Your elegant post might just spark the next big social media trend!

Why participate?

- Showcase your exquisite taste and inspire a wide audience.
- Gain the opportunity to be featured by StudioLux for greater visibility and recognition.

And there's more to come...

CLAIM YOUR EXCLUSIVE GIFTS!

To celebrate your creativity, we've designed an exclusive bonus filled with practical and inspiring ideas you can immediately use to enhance your home's style. Don't miss this special opportunity—it's your next step toward achieving interior excellence.

Follow these simple steps to claim your reward:

1. Capture your unique photo or create a compelling video featuring the book.
2. Share your creation on Instagram, TikTok, or Facebook using the hashtag #StudioLux.
3. Scan the QR code below to instantly unlock your exclusive bonus content.

Your moment of viral fame awaits!
With style and appreciation,

StudioLux

INTRODUCTION

Japandi: Where Japanese Zen Meets Scandinavian Comfort

Japandi is not merely an interior design trend; it's a thoughtful and harmonious fusion of two profound design philosophies—Japanese Zen minimalism and Scandinavian warmth. This powerful combination is rooted in the mutual respect both traditions share for simplicity, functionality, and a deep connection to nature. Japandi's appeal lies in its ability to create spaces that not only exude tranquility but also invite genuine comfort—qualities increasingly sought after in our busy, modern lives.

As a designer who has spent decades refining homes across the globe, I've seen firsthand how interiors shape our emotions, behaviors, and daily experiences. Japandi is particularly compelling because it effortlessly blends visual serenity with everyday practicality. It doesn't demand austere emptiness nor excessive coziness. Instead, Japandi strikes a delicate, nuanced balance—creating environments where clarity of form and warmth of texture coexist gracefully.

At the heart of Japandi lies the Zen philosophy from Japan, celebrating minimalism, mindfulness, and harmony. Japanese Zen-inspired interiors are purposefully understated, emphasizing openness and simplicity. Each object within a Zen space serves a clear function and aesthetic purpose. Spaces intentionally showcase the beauty of imperfection, subtle asymmetry, and thoughtful restraint.

Scandinavian design, meanwhile, provides the warmth and practical comfort so essential to modern homes. Originating from the cold climates of Northern Europe, Scandinavian interiors embrace coziness, simplicity, and gentle functionality. There's an emphasis on natural materials, tactile textures, and soft, neutral colors that nurture calm and comfort in everyday life. When these two design philosophies merge, they form Japandi—a design language that is both tranquil and welcoming, minimal yet warm, precise yet subtly imperfect. This harmony is precisely what makes Japandi so appealing: it satisfies our deep human desire for balance.

In the pages ahead, you'll discover how to embody Japandi's elegance within your own home. You'll explore the key components of this style—understanding exactly how color, furniture, materials, and decor interact seamlessly to create spaces of gentle sophistication. We'll delve into the importance of intentionally selecting every object, prioritizing quality and purpose, and ensuring each item resonates personally.

By the end of this book, you'll have gained a profound appreciation for Japandi's delicate art of balanced simplicity. More importantly, you'll be empowered to create living spaces that speak quietly yet clearly, harmonizing emotional tranquility with visual comfort, and blending the best of Japanese Zen and Scandinavian warmth in your own personal sanctuary.

Philosophy of Balanced Simplicity

Japandi's magic resides deeply in its philosophy of balanced simplicity. While many interior design approaches chase trends, excess, or elaborate detail, Japandi gracefully steps back, teaching us the value of mindful restraint and intentional living. To truly understand and effectively apply Japandi design, it's essential to grasp its philosophical foundations clearly.

Zen: Mindfulness and Purpose

Rooted in Japanese Zen traditions, Japandi design adopts mindfulness as its guiding principle. Zen emphasizes living intentionally—each object you choose for your space should not only serve a practical purpose but also enhance emotional clarity. Nothing is accidental or extraneous in Zen-inspired interiors; everything exists deliberately to evoke calmness and meaningfulness

This mindful selection and placement mean that your home becomes a genuine reflection of your personal values rather than a repository for arbitrary items. Zen design prompts you to continuously question the purpose and necessity of each item in your environment—does it add genuine value, either practically or emotionally? If not, it doesn't belong.

Hygge: Scandinavian Warmth and Comfort

Balancing Zen's minimal mindfulness, Japandi incorporates the Scandinavian concept of "hygge" (pronounced "hoo-ga"), defined as comfort, warmth, and contentment derived from simple pleasures. Hygge emphasizes creating cozy, welcoming environments—spaces that nourish and comfort us. It advocates soft lighting, tactile textures, and intimate arrangements to encourage relaxation and foster connections among loved ones.

Integrating hygge principles ensures Japandi homes never feel stark or cold. Instead, warmth and intimacy become essential components of simplicity, making spaces feel genuinely inviting, comforting, and deeply human.

Embracing Imperfection: Wabi-Sabi Influence

Japandi philosophy also gently integrates the Japanese concept of "Wabi-Sabi," the acceptance and appreciation of imperfection and impermanence. Instead of seeking flawless perfection, Japandi invites you to embrace subtle irregularities, signs of age, and gentle wear as beautiful reflections of authentic life.
This approach manifests through handcrafted furniture, artisan ceramics, and natural materials. A slightly uneven ceramic bowl or a gently worn wooden chair is not seen as flawed but valued precisely because it reveals its unique story. Wabi-Sabi thus ensures interiors never feel overly clinical or impersonal—they remain deeply resonant and authentically beautiful.

Harmony with Nature

Central to Japandi's balanced simplicity is a profound respect for nature. The philosophy prioritizes eco-friendly materials and designs that seamlessly connect indoor spaces to the outdoors. Biophilic elements, natural materials, and earthy color palettes are deliberately chosen to strengthen this connection, providing emotional grounding and environmental consciousness.
When designed well, Japandi spaces allow occupants to feel intimately connected to the natural world, fostering mental tranquility and physical well-being. Nature becomes an essential partner in design, not simply an external reference.

Practical Guidance: Achieving Balanced Simplicity

Implementing Japandi's philosophy requires intentional, deliberate choices:

Evaluate Mindfully:
- Regularly assess objects in your home for genuine usefulness and emotional significance. Remove anything extraneous.

Select Intentionally:
- Prioritize furnishings, decor, and materials that promote tranquility, warmth, and authentic beauty. Invest in quality over quantity.

Curate Regularly:
- Edit your spaces frequently, preserving visual clarity, emotional warmth, and subtle imperfection.

This mindful, deliberate practice ensures your interiors maintain balanced simplicity, true to Japandi's philosophy, enriching your daily experience of home.
By truly understanding and embodying Japandi's philosophy, your living spaces transform into calm sanctuaries, authentically balanced between mindful clarity and comforting warmth—spaces thoughtfully designed to nourish, inspire, and comfort, day after day.

CHAPTER 11
ESSENCE OF JAPANDI

The Origins and Philosophy

To fully appreciate the essence of Japandi, it's crucial to journey back through history and explore how this captivating style was born. Japandi, the elegant blend of Japanese Zen and Scandinavian minimalism, emerged organically rather than from deliberate intention. It reflects centuries of cultural evolution, merging the serenity and mindfulness of Eastern aesthetics with the comfort and practicality cherished in Northern European homes.

Historical Roots: Japanese Minimalism

Japanese design philosophy traces its roots back thousands of years, deeply influenced by Zen Buddhism, a tradition emphasizing mindfulness, contemplation, and the beauty of simplicity. Zen monks practiced living deliberately—each action mindful, every object meaningful. From tea ceremonies to carefully tended gardens, the Japanese cultivated an aesthetic language that celebrated the beauty inherent in restraint and intentionality.

The Japanese also introduced the concept of "Ma"—the beauty of negative space. Rather than seeing emptiness as lacking, "Ma" regards empty space as essential, creating visual calm and fostering mental tranquility.

Scandinavian Heritage: Comfort and Functionality

Halfway across the world, Scandinavian design principles emerged in Northern Europe around the early-to-mid 20th century. With long, harsh winters, Nordic homes prioritized warmth, practicality, and comfort. The Scandinavians developed a distinctive aesthetic that seamlessly blended functionality with elegant simplicity, where every item served a clear purpose yet exuded genuine warmth and charm.

The Danish concept "hygge" became fundamental—an untranslatable word meaning coziness, comfort, and intimate contentment derived from life's simplest pleasures. Scandinavian interiors prominently featured natural wood, soft textiles, gentle lighting, and muted, warm tones that evoked a deep sense of physical and emotional comfort.

The Emergence of Japandi

The fusion known today as Japandi naturally developed as designers worldwide recognized parallels and complementarity between Japanese Zen minimalism and Scandinavian warmth. Both styles inherently valued simplicity, nature, and mindful living, yet each offered something distinctively appealing to balance the other. Japanese interiors provided the discipline of visual restraint, symmetry, and emotional calmness, while Scandinavian designs contributed warmth, comfort, and accessible simplicity. This mutual enhancement gradually evolved into Japandi—a style uniquely suited to modern homes, blending Eastern tranquility and Western practicality.

Core Philosophical Influences

Two key philosophical foundations profoundly influence Japandi design:

Zen Mindfulness (Japan):
- Zen emphasizes awareness, intentionality, and tranquility. It encourages careful thought about each object's placement, purpose, and emotional resonance. Spaces designed with Zen mindfulness evoke mental clarity, peace, and serenity.

Hygge Comfort (Scandinavia):
- "Hygge" seeks to create inviting environments that soothe, comfort, and welcome. Soft textiles, warm colors, cozy furnishings, and thoughtful lighting arrangements characterize hygge spaces, ensuring emotional warmth and practical livability.

The intentional blending of these philosophies enables Japandi interiors to foster both mental tranquility and emotional comfort—an ideal combination rarely found in other design styles.

Integrating the Philosophy in Your Home

To authentically apply Japandi philosophy at home, consider these foundational guidelines:

Prioritize Intentionality:
- Evaluate each item for functionality and emotional significance. Choose pieces that genuinely resonate with your daily life and inner peace.

Balance Comfort and Minimalism:
- Select furniture and decor that is both practically comfortable and visually minimal. Neither comfort nor simplicity should dominate; rather, they should coexist harmoniously.

Embrace Imperfection:
- Integrate handcrafted or slightly aged objects, showcasing authenticity and subtle imperfection to add character, warmth, and visual richness.

Respect Negative Space ("Ma"):
- Arrange interiors thoughtfully, maintaining ample negative space around furnishings and decor. Empty space enhances visual harmony, serenity, and clarity.

By deeply understanding Japandi's historical origins and philosophical foundations, you can confidently transform your spaces into beautifully balanced environments. Your home thus becomes a genuine reflection of mindfulness, comfort, and simplicity—an elegant tribute to centuries of Eastern and Western wisdom combined into one timeless style.

Core Principles: Simplicity, Functionality, Comfort

Japandi design resonates deeply because it's founded on three enduring principles: simplicity, functionality, and comfort. These concepts are not merely decorative guidelines—they're vital philosophies that shape genuinely harmonious and livable interiors. By fully understanding and thoughtfully applying these principles, your home will effortlessly embody the elegance, practicality, and warmth that define authentic Japandi spaces.

Simplicity: The Power of Less

Simplicity is the heart of Japandi. It goes beyond minimal aesthetics—it's about intentional restraint and clarity of vision. Japandi interiors are thoughtfully curated spaces, free from clutter and visual chaos, where each piece of furniture and every decorative object has a clearly defined purpose.

When designing your Japandi-inspired space, consider simplicity as a form of refinement:

Curate Carefully:
- Select fewer, higher-quality items rather than many mediocre ones. Each object should be meaningful and thoughtfully placed.

Respect Negative Space:
- Utilize empty areas intentionally, allowing rooms to breathe visually. Negative space highlights the beauty and significance of each carefully chosen piece.

Neutral and Calm Color Schemes:
- Opt for muted palettes—soft whites, grays, warm neutrals—creating serene, calm backdrops.

Functionality: Practical Elegance

Functionality in Japandi isn't merely utilitarian—it's about thoughtfully designed elegance. Every furniture item and design decision serves a clear, practical purpose, enhancing daily life and simplifying routines. Japandi interiors avoid unnecessary complexity, ensuring rooms remain intuitive, accessible, and beautifully usable. Here's how to emphasize functionality in your Japandi interior:

Practical Furniture Choices:
- Select furniture with built-in storage, modular designs, or multi-purpose features—such as benches with hidden compartments or tables with extendable surfaces.

Logical Layouts:
- Arrange your furniture intuitively, ensuring easy movement and accessibility. Keep frequently used items within comfortable reach.

Durable, Quality Materials:
- Prioritize high-quality, long-lasting materials like solid wood, natural stone, and durable textiles that withstand daily use beautifully, enhancing functionality and aesthetic longevity.

Comfort: Warmth and Serenity

Comfort in Japandi interiors ensures spaces feel genuinely inviting, warm, and nurturing. Japandi never sacrifices comfort for aesthetic purity; rather, comfort complements simplicity and functionality, resulting in harmonious environments ideal for daily living. Enhance comfort effectively by:

Layering Textures:
- Introduce cozy, tactile textiles such as soft linen, wool rugs, plush throws, and comfortable upholstery.

Soft Lighting:
- Prioritize warm, layered lighting solutions. Gentle ambient lamps, elegant sconces, and subtle recessed lighting create welcoming atmospheres.

Organic Warmth:
- Integrate natural elements such as wooden furniture, indoor plants, and artisan ceramics. These organic touches subtly elevate emotional comfort.

Harmonizing the Principles

While simplicity, functionality, and comfort each hold distinctive importance, Japandi's true beauty emerges through their seamless integration. The principles must coexist effortlessly, ensuring each complements rather than conflicts with the others.

In practice, this harmony looks like:

- A minimalist sofa (simplicity) crafted with durable materials and practical built-in storage (functionality), dressed with soft, luxurious cushions (comfort).
- A clean-lined dining table (simplicity) crafted from high-quality oak for durability (functionality), paired with ergonomically shaped chairs upholstered in warm, tactile fabrics (comfort).

By fully embracing and harmonizing Japandi's core principles—simplicity, functionality, and comfort—you'll create spaces that are not only visually stunning but deeply enriching and genuinely welcoming. Your home becomes a sophisticated, serene retreat, perfectly balanced to support a mindful, comfortable, and beautifully uncomplicated lifestyle.

A Harmonious Color Palette: Neutrals and Soft Tones

A well-chosen color palette is fundamental in achieving the calming, harmonious aesthetic at the heart of Japandi design. Rather than vivid hues or stark contrasts, Japandi interiors embrace neutrals and soft, muted tones. These palettes foster emotional tranquility and visual cohesion, enhancing the subtle beauty of simplicity and craftsmanship found within each carefully curated room.

Why Neutrals and Soft Tones?

Neutral colors offer a gentle yet powerful way to anchor interiors, allowing other elements—textures, shapes, craftsmanship—to stand out gracefully. Soft, muted tones foster emotional calmness and visual serenity, creating inviting, restful spaces rather than visually overwhelming ones.

The subtlety of these tones also facilitates a seamless blend between the Zen minimalism of Japan and the cozy warmth of Scandinavian design. Each color quietly communicates a sense of naturalness, comfort, and timeless elegance.

Selecting the Perfect Japandi Colors

To achieve authentic Japandi color harmony, focus on these essential tones:

Warm Whites & Creams:
These tones reflect soft daylight beautifully, adding warmth and a subtle glow without harshness. They provide the perfect base color, creating airy, open spaces that feel calm and serene.

Gentle Greys & Taupes:
Greys and taupes introduce subtle depth and sophistication, creating spaces that feel refined yet welcoming. These shades beautifully complement natural materials like wood, stone, and textiles, enhancing visual texture and warmth.

Muted Earth Tones:
Soft earthy colors such as gentle sage green, pale olive, muted terracotta, and light sand tones evoke the natural world, adding quiet, organic warmth to interiors. They harmonize perfectly with Japandi's strong emphasis on nature and comfort.

Pale Pastels:
In controlled doses, pale pastels like blush, powdery blue, or soft lavender add delicate visual interest without disturbing the palette's tranquility. They are excellent choices for bedrooms, bathrooms, or relaxation spaces.

Achieving Visual Balance Through Color

In Japandi interiors, visual balance is crucial. Maintain harmony by considering these guidelines:

Dominant Base Color (60% Rule):
- Choose a warm white or soft neutral tone for walls and larger surfaces, setting a calm foundation for your space.

Secondary Color (30% Rule):
- Introduce a complementary neutral or gentle earthy tone—such as grey, taupe, or sage green—for furniture, cabinetry, or large decor elements, creating depth without visual clutter.

Accent Color (10% Rule):
- Incorporate a subtle pastel or muted tone sparingly for decorative elements, textiles, or small furnishings, enhancing visual interest delicately.

This balanced approach ensures the space remains visually cohesive, calm, and authentically Japandi.

Color and Natural Materials

Japandi design places enormous value on natural materials. Therefore, your color palette must harmonize seamlessly with wood tones, natural stone, bamboo, linen, wool, and other organic textures. Choose neutral tones that complement the natural warmth of wood grains—soft creams, taupes, and warm greys pair beautifully with oak, walnut, and ash. Muted greens and gentle earth tones enhance the beauty of ceramics, stone, and organic textiles, reinforcing the natural connection vital to Japandi interiors.

Harmonizing Color with Lighting

Natural daylight and warm artificial lighting dramatically influence how your chosen color palette is perceived. Japandi spaces thrive in soft, natural daylight, enhanced by strategically placed warm lighting.

When selecting colors:
- Test paint samples at various times of day to ensure harmony with changing natural light.
- Opt for lighting fixtures with warm LED bulbs (2700K-3000K) to maintain the palette's warmth and softness during evenings and darker days.

By thoughtfully embracing neutral and soft tones and carefully balancing them within your interiors, you create Japandi spaces of genuine tranquility, warmth, and timeless elegance. This harmonious color palette enhances simplicity, supports emotional comfort, and reinforces the inherent beauty of natural materials, achieving interiors that inspire genuine peace and sophisticated luxury.

CHAPTER 12
NATURAL MATERIALS AND TEXTURES

Embracing Wood: Authenticity and Warmth

In Japandi design, wood is much more than just a structural material; it's the soul of authenticity, warmth, and timeless elegance. Its natural beauty effortlessly bridges the serene minimalism of Japanese interiors with the welcoming comfort of Scandinavian homes, making it an essential element in crafting luxurious yet mindful living spaces.

Why Wood Matters in Japandi

Wood's unique appeal lies in its organic character, which embodies simplicity and authenticity. Its textures, grain patterns, and subtle imperfections resonate deeply with Japandi's core principles. Choosing wood isn't just about aesthetics—it's also about inviting nature indoors, creating spaces that feel emotionally grounding, inviting, and deeply comforting.

Wood also supports sustainability. Responsibly sourced or reclaimed wood aligns perfectly with Japandi's philosophy of mindful consumption and lasting quality.

Choosing the Right Wood

Selecting the right wood involves considering aesthetics, durability, and emotional warmth. Here are some ideal choices for luxurious Japandi interiors:

- Oak: Durable, versatile, and elegantly textured, oak blends strength with warmth, offering a balanced presence perfect for furniture, flooring, and cabinetry.
- Walnut: Known for its rich color and distinctive grain, walnut adds refined sophistication, ideal for accent furniture or statement pieces.
- Ash: Light in color and subtly textured, ash conveys delicate elegance and is excellent for creating airy, bright interiors.
- Teak: Naturally resilient and beautifully grained, teak is perfect for both indoor and outdoor settings, providing organic warmth and exceptional durability.

Each wood species offers distinct aesthetics and functional benefits, allowing tailored choices for specific spaces and design goals.

Incorporating Wood Thoughtfully

To maximize wood's aesthetic and emotional benefits, carefully integrate it into your Japandi spaces:

Statement Furniture:
- Use finely crafted wooden furniture as room anchors, such as a sculptural dining table, elegant lounge chairs, or minimalist bed frames. These pieces offer warmth and visual harmony.

Architectural Details:
- Incorporate wooden elements like exposed beams, wall paneling, or elegant staircases. These architectural features add natural authenticity and emotional depth.

Flooring Choices:
- Hardwood floors, especially wide-plank styles, set a serene and harmonious backdrop, providing subtle warmth and timeless elegance.

Accessories and Decor:
- Thoughtfully include smaller wooden objects—bowls, trays, lamps, or artisanal sculptures—to add tactile warmth and visual interest.

Finishes and Treatments: Enhancing Natural Beauty

The treatment of wood significantly influences its visual impact. To authentically reflect Japandi principles, favor subtle finishes that highlight wood's natural characteristics:

Matte or Satin Finishes:
- These gently enhance wood's natural beauty without overpowering its innate texture, color, and grain.

Oils and Waxes:
- Natural oils and waxes nourish the wood, deepening its color and enhancing its durability while allowing it to age gracefully over time.

Minimal or Natural Stains:
- When color adjustments are necessary, opt for subtle stains or treatments that preserve wood's authentic appearance rather than masking it.

Avoid glossy or overly polished finishes, as these detract from the organic, authentic aesthetic central to Japandi.

Wood and Sustainability: A Responsible Choice

Sustainability is integral to Japandi. Choosing sustainably harvested, reclaimed, or FSC-certified wood supports environmental responsibility and aligns with Japandi's mindful philosophy:

Sustainably Sourced Wood:
- Look for FSC (Forest Stewardship Council) certified wood, ensuring ethical forestry practices.

Reclaimed and Antique Wood:
- Embrace reclaimed wood with authentic patinas and unique stories, contributing to an environmentally conscious, emotionally resonant interior.

Local and Regional Sources:
- Prioritize local wood species, reducing transport-related environmental impacts and fostering stronger connections to your local environment.

These responsible choices ensure your Japandi interiors remain luxurious, authentic, and ethically sound.

Maintaining Wood: Beauty That Lasts

Wood requires thoughtful care to maintain its beauty and longevity. To care for wood in your Japandi home:

Regular Cleaning:
- Gently dust and clean wood surfaces with a soft, dry cloth, or occasionally with mild, natural cleaning products.

Routine Conditioning:
- Periodically treat wood with natural oils or waxes, protecting it from drying, cracking, and environmental changes.

Mindful Usage:
- Use protective coasters or pads for items like cups and vases, preventing unwanted marks and maintaining your wooden pieces' pristine condition.

Proper maintenance ensures your wooden elements remain beautiful and comforting for generations, genuinely reflecting Japandi's enduring appeal.

By thoughtfully embracing wood's authenticity and warmth, you anchor your Japandi interiors in emotional depth, timeless elegance, and serene luxury. Each wooden element carefully chosen and maintained enhances the space's visual beauty and spiritual resonance, deeply connecting your home to the natural world and the mindful, comforting principles of Japandi design.

Bamboo: Strength and Flexibility

Within the refined aesthetic of Japandi, bamboo holds a special place—not only for its visual appeal but for the philosophical symbolism it brings into interiors. Celebrated for its exceptional strength, graceful flexibility, and rapid sustainability, bamboo seamlessly merges Japanese reverence for natural materials with Scandinavian practicality and innovation.

Bamboo in Japandi: Beyond Aesthetics

Bamboo's appeal in Japandi design extends well beyond its visual charm. Its presence introduces both strength and delicacy, representing resilience and adaptability—qualities deeply valued in Japanese philosophy. As an incredibly fast-growing and sustainable material, bamboo perfectly aligns with Scandinavian ideals of practicality and ecological responsibility, making it a quintessential choice for contemporary luxury Japandi homes.

The Strength of Bamboo: Durable Elegance

Despite its light and delicate appearance, bamboo is astonishingly robust and resilient. When properly harvested and treated, bamboo rivals hardwoods in durability and longevity, providing both structural strength and lasting beauty.

Common applications of bamboo in Japandi design include:

Flooring:
- Bamboo flooring offers exceptional durability, resistance to wear, and beautiful, subtle grain patterns. Its natural hues, from pale straw to warm caramel tones, complement neutral Japandi interiors seamlessly.

Furniture:
- Bamboo furniture, including tables, chairs, and shelving, offers elegant, lightweight structures with impressive strength. Its natural flexibility allows artisans to craft graceful, gently curved shapes that harmonize beautifully within minimalist spaces.

Architectural Features:
- Structural elements, such as screens, partitions, or decorative wall paneling, harness bamboo's strength and visual subtlety, creating dynamic yet understated architectural focal points.

The Flexibility of Bamboo: Graceful Versatility

One of bamboo's most remarkable qualities is its inherent flexibility, enabling graceful forms and intricate details. Bamboo's pliability makes it ideal for weaving or crafting delicate furniture, lighting fixtures, and decorative elements that enrich Japandi interiors with soft, elegant curves.
Examples of bamboo flexibility in Japandi design include:

Lighting Fixtures:
- Bamboo pendant lights, lanterns, and lampshades showcase intricate weaving and organic shapes, offering warm, diffused lighting ideal for creating soft, comforting atmospheres.

Decorative Elements:
- Subtle bamboo baskets, trays, and woven panels provide gentle, tactile warmth and visual interest without overwhelming Japandi's minimalist serenity.

Room Dividers and Screens:
- Beautifully crafted bamboo screens, inspired by traditional Japanese "shoji" partitions, offer elegant and functional ways to create private, serene spaces while maintaining visual openness.

Sustainability: A Rapidly Renewable Resource

Bamboo's rapid growth makes it one of the most environmentally responsible choices for modern interiors. Mature bamboo can be harvested in just a few years—far quicker than conventional hardwood trees, which require decades. This rapid renewability aligns perfectly with Japandi's ethical commitment to environmental mindfulness and sustainable luxury.

When selecting bamboo products, prioritize:

Responsibly Harvested Bamboo:
- Choose bamboo sourced from environmentally responsible plantations, certified by recognized sustainable forestry standards.

Non-toxic Treatments:
- Opt for bamboo treated with natural, non-toxic finishes and adhesives, ensuring your interiors remain safe, healthy, and environmentally friendly.

Local Artisans:
- Whenever possible, support local artisans or reputable international suppliers who follow transparent, ethical harvesting and production practices.

Caring for Bamboo: Longevity and Beauty

Maintaining bamboo's elegant appearance and impressive durability is straightforward with mindful care:

Regular Cleaning:
- Dust bamboo surfaces regularly and wipe clean using a damp cloth with mild, eco-friendly soap. Avoid harsh chemicals that could damage bamboo's natural finish.

Preventive Care:
- Use pads or coasters beneath heavy or sharp objects to protect bamboo surfaces from dents and scratches. Avoid prolonged direct sunlight, as excessive exposure can fade bamboo's natural color over time.

Routine Maintenance:
- Periodically apply natural oils or wax treatments specifically formulated for bamboo, maintaining its vibrant appearance and structural integrity.

Integrating bamboo thoughtfully into your Japandi interiors enhances not only visual elegance but also emotional resonance and environmental integrity. With its remarkable strength, graceful flexibility, and extraordinary sustainability, bamboo embodies the essence of Japandi—combining the quiet sophistication of Japanese design with the practical warmth of Scandinavian interiors, resulting in luxurious spaces that feel genuinely harmonious, ethically responsible, and deeply serene.

Stone and Ceramics: Quiet Beauty and Imperfection

In the thoughtfully restrained world of Japandi design, stone and ceramics play a uniquely poetic role. Each embodies quiet beauty, celebrates natural imperfections, and contributes to an interior's tranquil elegance. The harmonious interplay of these materials introduces emotional depth, subtle texture, and timeless sophistication, vital in creating spaces that truly resonate with the essence of Japandi.

Stone: Timeless Elegance and Natural Authenticity

Stone, a material with enduring appeal, brings profound authenticity and graceful permanence to Japandi interiors. Its inherent variations, subtle textures, and understated strength create a deep connection to the natural world, aligning seamlessly with Japandi's minimalist yet warm philosophy.
Ideal Stone Choices for Japandi Interiors:

Marble:
- With gentle veins and muted tones, honed marble introduces quiet sophistication, providing visual depth without overwhelming the minimalist aesthetic.

Travertine and Limestone:
- These softer, earthy stones offer serene textures and natural warmth, ideal for flooring, countertops, or subtle architectural features.

Slate and Granite:
- Darker, subtly textured stones like slate or matte granite add visual interest and grounding contrast, complementing soft, neutral palettes elegantly.

Integrating Stone Thoughtfully:
Surfaces and Flooring:
- Stone flooring or kitchen and bathroom surfaces provide tactile richness, quiet luxury, and effortless durability, enhancing daily experiences.

Feature Walls:
- A carefully selected stone feature wall introduces a compelling focal point, quietly anchoring the space and emphasizing natural texture.

Decorative Objects:
- Stone bowls, trays, or sculptural elements subtly celebrate organic beauty and mindful craftsmanship, enhancing visual serenity.

Ceramics: Celebrating Imperfection and Artisan Craftsmanship

Handcrafted ceramics are inherently aligned with Japandi's appreciation for subtle imperfections, authentic craftsmanship, and emotional resonance. Each ceramic object—whether a vase, bowl, or vessel—tells a story through its unique shape, glaze, and gentle irregularities, perfectly embodying the Japanese concept of "Wabi-Sabi."
Ideal Ceramics for Japandi Spaces:

Hand-thrown Pottery:
- Artisanal bowls, plates, and vessels exhibit gentle asymmetry, distinctive glazes, and subtle imperfections, enriching interiors with character and warmth.

Minimalist Vases:
- Simple, sculptural ceramic vases provide understated elegance, beautifully complementing minimal floral or botanical arrangements.

Ceramic Lighting:
- Handmade ceramic lamps or pendants with soft finishes and gentle shapes create warm, inviting atmospheres through tactile illumination.

Displaying Ceramics Thoughtfully:

Minimalist Groupings:
- Arrange ceramics sparingly, using groupings of three or five items to create visual harmony and emphasize each piece's quiet beauty.

Functional Aesthetics:
- Incorporate ceramics as functional decor—tableware, kitchen storage, bathroom accessories—enhancing daily activities with aesthetic mindfulness.

Artistic Showcase:
- Position striking ceramics as focal points on shelves, consoles, or coffee tables, allowing their craftsmanship and imperfections to shine.

Embracing Wabi-Sabi: Beauty in Imperfection

Both stone and ceramics naturally exemplify the Japanese philosophy of "Wabi-Sabi"—the appreciation of transience, imperfection, and authentic beauty. Japandi design actively celebrates these qualities rather than attempting to conceal them:

Patina and Aging:
- Welcome gentle aging in stone surfaces—minor etching, subtle wear—as signs of natural beauty rather than flaws.

Glaze Variations and Crackling:
- Cherish handcrafted ceramics' slight glaze variations, gentle color shifts, or fine "crazing" (crackled glazing). These perceived imperfections enrich emotional resonance and aesthetic depth.

Authentic Touches:
- Emphasize ceramics and stone crafted by artisans, ensuring each piece carries a genuine, human-made quality.

Caring for Stone and Ceramics: Mindful Maintenance

Maintaining these materials is straightforward with intentional care:

Stone Care:
- Regularly clean stone surfaces gently using mild, eco-friendly products. Occasionally seal porous stones like marble or limestone to protect against stains and maintain their subtle elegance.

Ceramic Care:
- Dust ceramics regularly, hand-wash functional pieces with gentle detergents, and avoid abrasive cleaning methods that could harm delicate glazes.

By thoughtfully incorporating stone and ceramics into your Japandi interiors, you craft spaces of quiet luxury, emotional authenticity, and timeless beauty. Each carefully selected and intentionally placed element subtly contributes to a serene and deeply meaningful environment, gracefully celebrating imperfection, craftsmanship, and natural authenticity—the heart of Japandi's enduring charm.

Soft Textiles: Linen, Wool, Cotton

In Japandi interiors, textiles are quietly powerful. They possess the unique ability to introduce warmth, texture, and comfort without disturbing the simplicity and clarity central to the style. Carefully chosen fabrics such as linen, wool, and cotton subtly enhance a space's emotional warmth, tactile appeal, and inviting softness, all essential to creating luxurious yet serene Japandi environments.

The Role of Textiles in Japandi Design

Japandi textiles aren't mere decorative accents; they're purposeful elements integral to achieving emotional comfort and refined simplicity. Soft textiles balance minimalist aesthetics by providing warmth and comfort, transforming interiors into genuinely nurturing, inviting sanctuaries. Their natural fibers, subtle textures, and muted colors echo Japandi's dedication to nature, authenticity, and quiet beauty.

Linen: Natural Elegance and Breezy Comfort

Linen is particularly beloved in Japandi design, praised for its refined texture, natural breathability, and graceful drape. Derived from flax, linen effortlessly complements minimalist interiors with its understated yet distinctly luxurious character.

Benefits of Linen:
- Breathability: Linen's naturally airy weave regulates temperature, ideal for bedding, curtains, and upholstery.
- Texture and Drape: Its softly structured appearance introduces subtle depth and visual interest without overwhelming minimal spaces.
- Sustainability: Linen is environmentally friendly—highly renewable, biodegradable, and often produced sustainably.

How to Incorporate Linen:
- Bedding and Curtains: Linen sheets, duvet covers, or curtains add relaxed luxury, fostering serene, restful atmospheres.
- Upholstery and Cushion Covers: Linen-upholstered furniture or decorative pillows provide visual softness and tactile comfort.

Wool: Cozy Warmth and Tactile Luxury

Wool introduces essential warmth and soft, tactile richness to Japandi interiors, especially valuable in colder climates. Derived from natural fibers, wool symbolizes comfort, hygge, and timeless quality.

Benefits of Wool:
- Insulation and Warmth: Wool naturally insulates, making it perfect for rugs, blankets, and throws that add visual warmth and emotional comfort.
- Durability: Wool fibers are resilient, maintaining beauty and functionality through years of use.
- Natural Texture: Wool's gentle texture complements Japandi's soft neutrals, adding subtle visual depth.

How to Incorporate Wool:
- Rugs and Carpets: Woolen rugs anchor seating areas, providing physical and emotional warmth, softness, and comfort.
- Throws and Blankets: Draped wool blankets or knitted throws introduce hygge-inspired coziness, inviting relaxed intimacy.

Cotton: Softness, Practicality, and Versatility

Cotton is an essential Japandi textile due to its versatile softness, everyday practicality, and visual simplicity. Its understated elegance perfectly aligns with Japandi's functional yet comfortable philosophy.

Benefits of Cotton:
- Soft and Comfortable: Cotton's gentle softness makes it ideal for daily-use items like bedding, towels, and upholstery.
- Easy Care: Cotton is durable, machine-washable, and effortlessly maintainable, reflecting Japandi's preference for functional luxury.
- Subtle Texture: Cotton provides visual softness without distracting from minimalist aesthetics, seamlessly integrating into neutral palettes.

How to Incorporate Cotton:
- Towels and Bath Linens: Plush cotton towels enhance bathroom luxury, blending comfort, functionality, and visual serenity.
- Upholstery and Decorative Pillows: Cotton fabrics on sofas, chairs, or pillows offer comfortable, practical luxury, perfect for everyday living spaces.

Balancing Texture and Simplicity

Effective Japandi textile integration requires balancing tactile richness with visual simplicity. Achieve this balance through:

Subtle Layering:
- Layer textiles gently—pair linen bedding with wool blankets or cotton upholstery with linen cushions, maintaining visual clarity while enriching tactile warmth.

Harmonious Color Choices:
- Select textiles in soft neutrals or muted tones that blend naturally, enhancing overall harmony rather than creating stark contrasts.

Thoughtful Placement:
- Incorporate textiles intentionally in areas emphasizing comfort and relaxation—bedrooms, living spaces, and cozy reading corners.

Caring for Your Textiles: Lasting Comfort

Maintaining these natural textiles is straightforward yet essential:

Gentle Cleaning:
- Follow fabric-specific care instructions, washing linens and cotton gently and professionally cleaning wool items periodically.

Proper Storage:
- Store textiles appropriately, folded neatly or hung properly, protecting them from excessive moisture, sunlight, and pests.

Regular Rotation:
- Rotate frequently used textiles (cushions, throws, bedding) to distribute wear evenly, preserving their longevity and beauty.

By thoughtfully selecting and integrating linen, wool, and cotton into your Japandi interiors, you craft spaces of unmatched softness, quiet elegance, and genuine comfort. These natural textiles become essential partners in creating harmonious, serene interiors, quietly enriching daily life with tactile luxury, emotional warmth, and timeless visual refinement.

CHAPTER 13
JAPANDI FURNITURE ESSENTIALS

Timeless Furniture Designs

In Japandi interiors, furniture is more than simply functional—it's foundational. Carefully selected furniture defines the character of the space, creating an enduring sense of tranquility, warmth, and sophistication. True Japandi furniture embodies timeless designs that resist trends, gracefully blending Japanese minimalism with Scandinavian comfort and practicality. Each piece thoughtfully chosen contributes quietly but profoundly to the serenity, luxury, and aesthetic harmony of your home.

Why Timelessness Matters in Japandi Furniture

Japandi's allure lies in its refined simplicity and emotional depth, characteristics inherently timeless. Furniture designed with longevity in mind offers lasting visual and emotional satisfaction, transcending fleeting trends or fashions. By prioritizing timeless pieces, your home maintains an enduring elegance, resonating deeply year after year.

Timeless furniture designs typically feature clean, simple lines, thoughtful proportions, subtle detailing, and exceptional craftsmanship. These attributes ensure longevity, both physically and aesthetically, making them essential investments for authentic Japandi interiors.

Essential Characteristics of Timeless Japandi Furniture

Understanding the distinctive qualities of timeless Japandi furniture empowers thoughtful selections for your home:

1. Clean and Simple Lines
Japandi furniture consistently exhibits clean, minimalist lines and uncomplicated forms. Each piece emphasizes clarity and visual calmness, without unnecessary ornamentation. This simplicity harmonizes seamlessly with other design elements, fostering serene interiors.

2. Natural and Authentic Materials
Wood, bamboo, stone, and natural fibers define Japandi furniture. These materials age gracefully, becoming more beautiful over time. Their inherent warmth and tactile qualities support emotional comfort and natural authenticity.

3. Functional Elegance
Functionality is never sacrificed for aesthetics. Each furniture piece combines practical features—hidden storage, ergonomic design, intuitive functionality—with subtle elegance, enhancing both usability and visual appeal.

4. Neutral and Muted Finishes
Furniture finishes in Japandi interiors prioritize subtlety. Matte, satin, or naturally oiled finishes showcase material beauty, texture, and craftsmanship without visual distraction or overwhelming glossiness.

Key Timeless Japandi Furniture Pieces

Several furniture types have become synonymous with the timeless essence of Japandi:

Low-Profile Seating:
Inspired by Japanese seating traditions, low-profile sofas, daybeds, and lounge chairs emphasize tranquility and comfort. These designs create intimate, grounded seating arrangements, fostering relaxation and calmness.

Minimalist Dining Tables:
Japandi dining tables feature restrained yet welcoming designs. Typically crafted from solid wood with gently rounded edges or subtle, geometric shapes, they combine simplicity with warmth and inviting comfort.

Multifunctional Storage Pieces:
Thoughtfully designed storage—such as built-in cabinetry, sideboards, or benches with hidden compartments—balance elegance with practicality, keeping interiors serene and uncluttered.

Timeless Accent Chairs:
Japandi accent chairs offer striking yet restrained designs, often incorporating organic shapes and fine craftsmanship. They serve as elegant focal points, enhancing both functionality and aesthetic interest.

Integrating Timeless Furniture Thoughtfully

Integrating timeless Japandi furniture effectively requires mindful consideration of these principles:

Balance and Proportion:
- Choose furniture proportional to your room size and spatial layout, ensuring visual harmony and comfort.

Intentional Placement:
- Position furniture intuitively, fostering comfortable conversation and movement flow, and maintaining visual openness through deliberate negative space.

Unified Aesthetic:
- Select pieces that complement each other aesthetically—harmonizing materials, colors, and styles—to create cohesive, emotionally resonant spaces.

Caring for Timeless Furniture: Preserving Beauty

Timeless furniture deserves careful maintenance to preserve its enduring elegance:

Routine Cleaning:
- Regularly dust surfaces and gently clean with mild, natural cleansers. Avoid harsh chemicals that damage finishes and materials.

Occasional Conditioning:
- Use natural oils or waxes to nourish and protect wooden or bamboo furniture, maintaining structural integrity and visual appeal.

Protective Measures:
- Utilize coasters, pads, and protective felt to guard furniture surfaces from damage, ensuring lasting beauty and functionality.

Investing in timeless Japandi furniture ensures that your interiors remain sophisticated, serene, and beautifully functional through the years. Each thoughtfully chosen piece contributes significantly to the emotional and visual harmony central to Japandi design, transforming your home into a genuinely timeless sanctuary of mindful luxury and refined comfort.

Balancing Japanese Minimalism and Scandinavian Warmth

The unique allure of Japandi lies in its thoughtful blending of two distinct design traditions: the serene precision of Japanese minimalism and the inviting warmth of Scandinavian comfort. Achieving a harmonious balance between these influences is key to creating interiors that are both visually elegant and genuinely welcoming. To master Japandi design, you must deeply understand how to combine Japanese clarity with Scandinavian coziness—each thoughtfully integrated to complement, rather than overpower, the other.

Understanding the Two Traditions

To achieve balance, begin by appreciating the core essence of each tradition separately:

Japanese Minimalism
- Visual Calm: Emphasis on open spaces, clean lines, and thoughtful emptiness.
- Purposeful Simplicity: Each item has a clear function, intentionally placed for maximum impact and clarity.
- Zen Principles: Focuses on mindfulness, tranquility, and emotional calmness.

Scandinavian Warmth
- Comfort and Practicality: Spaces prioritize ease of living, functional furniture, and inviting layouts.
- Soft Textures: Use of tactile fabrics, cozy rugs, and inviting upholstery for warmth.
- Hygge Philosophy: Encourages creating intimate environments, fostering relaxation and connection.

Understanding these distinct yet complementary philosophies allows you to integrate them effectively, creating rooms defined by visual serenity and tactile warmth.

Furniture Choices: Precision Meets Comfort

Japandi furniture selections should intentionally reflect both design traditions:

Minimalist Forms, Maximum Comfort:
- Opt for furniture that blends clean, minimalist lines with ergonomic comfort—such as a simple yet deeply comfortable sofa, or streamlined yet softly upholstered chairs.

Natural Warmth and Clarity:
- Select furniture crafted from natural materials like solid wood or bamboo, balancing visual minimalism with tactile richness.

Functional Elegance:
- Scandinavian multifunctional storage meets Japanese minimalist aesthetics—such as hidden storage benches, sleek cabinets, or low-profile shelving—to maintain visual serenity while offering practical solutions.

Lighting: Softening the Minimalist Aesthetic

Lighting plays a critical role in balancing Japandi interiors:

Warm, Layered Lighting:
- Combine Japanese-inspired minimal fixtures (simple pendant lamps, subtle recessed lighting) with Scandinavian-style soft ambient lighting (floor lamps, table lamps, candles).

Natural Daylight:
- Maximize natural light with sheer curtains or shoji-inspired screens, creating gentle, diffused daylight that softens and warms minimalist spaces.

Accessorizing with Intention

Accessories in Japandi interiors must enhance emotional comfort without cluttering visual simplicity:

Minimalist Decor with Warmth:
- Select artisanal ceramics, organic wooden objects, or subtle botanical elements—carefully curated to add emotional warmth without visual distraction.

Textural Contrasts:
- Pair smooth surfaces (Japanese lacquer, polished stone) with tactile, organic textures (woven baskets, knitted throws), creating subtle yet engaging visual interest.

Limited but Meaningful:
- Restrict decorative elements to a few meaningful items, ensuring each piece contributes positively to emotional comfort and visual harmony.

Practical Guidance for Perfect Balance

Achieving the ideal Japandi balance involves thoughtful practice:

Evaluate Regularly:
- Regularly assess spaces, adjusting items or layouts as necessary to maintain harmony and visual simplicity.

Comfort Check:
- Ensure each room feels genuinely comfortable to use—test seating comfort, lighting warmth, and textile softness regularly.

Visual Clarity:
- Continuously refine your interiors, eliminating unnecessary visual clutter while adding subtle elements to maintain warmth and welcoming comfort.

Balancing Japanese minimalism and Scandinavian warmth results in interiors uniquely elegant, thoughtfully inviting, and genuinely serene. By mastering this subtle balance, you craft spaces that celebrate the quiet beauty of restraint alongside the nurturing power of comfort—truly embodying Japandi's enduring appeal.

Craftsmanship and Sustainable Materials

In Japandi design, furniture and decor are not only chosen for their visual appeal or comfort—they are also thoughtfully selected based on their craftsmanship, ethical production, and environmental sustainability. This intentional approach ensures each piece brings genuine beauty, lasting quality, and profound meaning into your interiors. Understanding and prioritizing craftsmanship and sustainable materials is essential for authentically embodying Japandi's philosophy of mindful, luxurious living.

Craftsmanship: Honoring Artistry and Authenticity

Japandi deeply values craftsmanship. It cherishes objects made with skill, care, and genuine passion—qualities that elevate furniture and decor far beyond simple aesthetics. Craftsmanship introduces emotional depth, subtle sophistication, and timeless durability, transforming your interiors into spaces of authentic luxury and meaningful connection.

Why Craftsmanship Matters:
- Quality and Longevity: Expertly crafted pieces last generations, resisting trends and providing long-term satisfaction.
- Emotional Resonance: Handmade or artisan-crafted items carry emotional stories and human warmth, deeply enriching interior spaces.
- Subtle Imperfection: Craftsmanship introduces subtle imperfections and unique details, echoing the Japanese philosophy of Wabi-Sabi—beauty found in authenticity and imperfection.

Identifying Quality Craftsmanship:
- Visible Joinery: Look for precision joinery in furniture—such as dovetail, mortise-and-tenon, or finger joints—demonstrating skilled, durable construction.
- Refined Finishing: Quality craftsmanship is evident in smooth finishes, elegant detailing, and thoughtfully applied materials.
- Artisan Signature: Handcrafted objects often bear subtle markers of their makers, enhancing authenticity and emotional value.

Sustainable Materials: Ethical Luxury and Lasting Quality

Japandi's commitment to sustainability goes beyond environmental awareness; it's a conscious choice that reflects personal values, responsibility, and long-term vision. Sustainable materials ensure your interiors are not only beautiful but also ethically sound, environmentally responsible, and genuinely luxurious.

Preferred Sustainable Materials for Japandi:
Responsibly Harvested Wood:
- FSC-certified or locally sourced woods guarantee ethical harvesting and minimal environmental impact. Oak, ash, walnut, or reclaimed timber exemplify luxurious, sustainable options.

Bamboo:
- Rapidly renewable, bamboo offers excellent sustainability without compromising strength, beauty, or flexibility.

Natural Textiles:
- Linen, wool, cotton, and hemp—all natural, renewable fibers—provide sustainable comfort and elegance while minimizing chemical use and environmental impact.

Stone and Ceramics:
- Locally sourced stone or artisan-produced ceramics embody long-lasting durability, reducing frequent replacements and unnecessary waste.

Selecting Ethical and Sustainable Pieces

To thoughtfully incorporate sustainable craftsmanship into your Japandi interiors, follow these essential considerations:
- Transparent Sourcing:
- Prioritize brands and artisans transparently sharing information about material sourcing, production processes, and sustainability practices.
- Local and Artisan-Made:
- Choose locally made products to support community artisans and reduce transportation-related environmental impacts, simultaneously fostering economic sustainability.
- Timeless Design:
- Opt for furniture and decor featuring timeless aesthetics and superior craftsmanship, ensuring long-term satisfaction and reduced waste through lasting quality.

Caring for Your Crafted Pieces: Ensuring Longevity

Proper care preserves the beauty, functionality, and sustainability of well-crafted furniture and decor:

- Routine Maintenance:
- Regularly dust and clean furniture gently using natural cleaning solutions. Maintain finishes with appropriate natural oils or waxes.
- Preventive Protection:
- Use coasters, felt pads, and protective mats to prevent accidental damage to surfaces, preserving their refined appearance and structural integrity.
- Professional Restoration:
- When necessary, professionally restore rather than replace cherished items, honoring craftsmanship and sustainability commitments.

Integrating Craftsmanship and Sustainability in Japandi Interiors

Authentic Japandi design carefully integrates craftsmanship and sustainable materials into every aspect of your interiors:

Furniture:

- Select furniture meticulously crafted from sustainably harvested woods or bamboo, ensuring both ethical sourcing and enduring beauty.

Textiles:

- Choose natural, sustainably produced textiles, prioritizing artisanal craftsmanship and quality over mass-produced options.

Decor:

- Curate ceramics, stone objects, and handcrafted accessories intentionally, each chosen for sustainable practices, skilled craftsmanship, and timeless appeal.

By consciously prioritizing craftsmanship and sustainable materials in your Japandi spaces, you elevate your home's aesthetic, emotional resonance, and ethical integrity. Your interiors become meaningful expressions of mindful luxury—spaces defined not only by visual beauty but also by thoughtful choices, skilled artistry, and responsible living. This holistic approach ensures your Japandi home remains beautiful, timeless, and genuinely sustainable, deeply reflecting your personal values and commitment to refined, conscious living.

Iconic Japandi Pieces: Chairs, Tables, Storage

In Japandi interiors, certain furniture items stand out as true icons. These essential pieces—chairs, tables, and storage solutions—are the foundation of any luxurious Japandi home, clearly expressing the style's distinct blend of Japanese minimalism and Scandinavian comfort. Selecting iconic Japandi furniture requires recognizing designs that embody simplicity, craftsmanship, functionality, and warmth. Each carefully chosen piece not only serves practical purposes but also enhances emotional tranquility and visual elegance.

Iconic Japandi Chairs: Elegant Comfort

Japandi chairs effortlessly combine graceful Japanese minimalism with Scandinavian ergonomic comfort. These chairs aren't merely seating—they're sculptural objects that quietly elevate interiors through refined aesthetics and inviting usability.

Key Features of Japandi Chairs:

Low and Grounded Forms:
- Influenced by traditional Japanese seating, these chairs offer grounded comfort and serene aesthetics.

Organic, Curved Lines:
- Curves enhance ergonomic comfort, subtly softening minimalist designs without visual clutter.

Natural Materials:
- Solid wood, bamboo, woven textiles, or fine leather are preferred for authentic warmth and tactile luxury.

Iconic Examples:

Wishbone Chair:
- A Scandinavian classic influenced by Asian forms, it embodies simple elegance with organic curves and skilled woodcraft.

Japanese-Inspired Lounge Chair:
- Low-profile chairs, with clean lines and soft upholstery, capture Zen tranquility and cozy warmth simultaneously.

Iconic Japandi Tables: Minimalist Functionality

Japandi tables epitomize restrained elegance and intuitive functionality. Designed to blend Japanese minimalism's visual clarity with Scandinavian practicality, these tables become focal points of daily life, grounding rooms with subtle warmth and purposeful simplicity.

Key Features of Japandi Tables:

Clean, Streamlined Forms:
- Simple yet elegant lines, minimal detailing, and balanced proportions define Japandi tables.

Quality Craftsmanship:
- Superior craftsmanship, especially visible joinery or subtle detailing, showcases timeless elegance and lasting quality.

Versatile Practicality:
- Extendable tables, nesting tables, or tables with subtle storage solutions exemplify functional minimalism and everyday usability.

Iconic Examples:
Low Wooden Coffee Table:
- Inspired by Japanese tea tables, it offers simple elegance, intuitive usability, and inviting warmth.

Solid Oak Dining Table:
- Scandinavian-crafted, sustainably sourced oak dining tables embody functional elegance and quiet visual harmony.

Iconic Japandi Storage: Elegant Practicality

Japandi storage pieces effortlessly blend Japanese precision and Scandinavian practicality. Carefully designed to maintain visual serenity while offering intuitive usability, these items ensure interiors remain uncluttered, organized, and elegantly minimal.

Key Features of Japandi Storage:

Hidden Functionality:
- Integrated or concealed storage maintains clean visual aesthetics, ensuring practicality without clutter.

Minimalist Design:
- Simple lines, subtle detailing, and seamless surfaces emphasize visual calmness and effortless functionality.

Natural Materials and Finishes:
- Sustainably sourced woods, natural textiles, and soft, matte finishes support Japandi's mindful luxury and emotional warmth.

Iconic Examples:

Japanese-inspired Sideboards:
- Sleek, minimalist cabinets featuring subtle sliding doors or hidden drawers provide discreet yet effective storage.

Scandinavian Multifunctional Benches:
- Elegant benches with integrated storage or soft seating offer functional beauty and practical luxury.

Curating Your Japandi Icons: Thoughtful Selection

Choosing iconic Japandi furniture for your interiors involves careful thought, balancing functionality, aesthetics, and emotional resonance:

Consider Your Needs:
- Choose furniture based on genuine lifestyle needs, prioritizing intuitive usability and everyday comfort.

Prioritize Quality and Craftsmanship:
- Invest in high-quality pieces crafted sustainably and ethically, ensuring long-lasting satisfaction and enduring elegance.

Harmonize Aesthetics:
- Ensure your chosen chairs, tables, and storage pieces harmonize visually, supporting overall simplicity, warmth, and balance in your interiors.

Caring for Your Japandi Furniture Icons

Ensure your iconic Japandi furniture pieces retain their beauty and functionality through mindful care:

Routine Maintenance:
- Regularly clean surfaces gently with eco-friendly products, maintaining materials' integrity and finishes' subtle elegance.

Preventive Care:
- Use protective pads, coasters, and thoughtful placement to prevent accidental damage and preserve lasting beauty.

Professional Restoration:
- Professionally restore rather than replace valued items, respecting craftsmanship, longevity, and sustainability principles.

By thoughtfully selecting and maintaining iconic Japandi chairs, tables, and storage solutions, your interiors will exemplify Japandi's refined, luxurious simplicity. These carefully chosen pieces create spaces that deeply resonate emotionally, visually, and practically, embodying Japandi's true spirit—balanced harmony, authentic comfort, and timeless elegance.

CHAPTER 14
JAPANDI LIVING SPACES

Creating Zen-inspired Living Rooms

A Zen-inspired living room is the essence of Japandi living: a space of serenity, refinement, and emotional clarity. This room serves as the peaceful heart of your home—a sanctuary thoughtfully designed for relaxation, mindfulness, and connection. Achieving this requires careful consideration of furniture, color, layout, and decor, thoughtfully blending minimalist Japanese aesthetics with inviting Scandinavian warmth. The result is a luxurious living room that promotes calmness and emotional well-being.

The Essence of a Zen-inspired Living Room

Zen-inspired spaces are deliberately quiet and uncluttered. They prioritize visual simplicity and emotional tranquility. Every element chosen should foster serenity, balance, and mindful living. Japandi living rooms achieve this effortlessly by blending gentle minimalism with subtle textures, warm neutrals, and carefully considered furniture arrangements.

Selecting Furniture for Serenity

Furniture is foundational in Zen-inspired Japandi living rooms. Choose pieces that balance visual minimalism with tangible comfort, focusing on these guidelines:

Low-Profile Furniture:
- Low seating arrangements—sofas, chairs, and coffee tables—create grounded, calming atmospheres inspired by traditional Japanese design.

Organic Forms and Clean Lines:
- Choose furniture with soft curves and minimalist silhouettes. Clean, simple lines ensure visual calmness, while gentle curves add warmth and inviting comfort.

Quality and Craftsmanship:
- Invest in expertly crafted furniture from natural materials like sustainably sourced wood, bamboo, or linen upholstery, supporting visual authenticity and lasting beauty.

Harmonious Color Palettes for Calmness

Zen-inspired Japandi living rooms favor muted, calming color palettes that evoke tranquility, balance, and subtle warmth:

Neutral Foundations:
- Choose soft whites, gentle grays, and warm beige tones for walls and larger furnishings, creating serene visual backdrops.

Earthy and Muted Accents:
- Introduce subtle earthy colors—sage green, muted taupe, gentle terracotta—for smaller furniture pieces, textiles, and decor, enhancing natural warmth without visual disruption.

Minimal Contrast:
- Keep color contrasts minimal and harmonious, ensuring interiors remain visually restful and emotionally calming.

Textural Warmth and Softness

Zen-inspired Japandi spaces rely heavily on textures to enhance visual interest without clutter:

Tactile Textiles:
- Layer cozy, tactile textiles such as linen, wool, or cotton throws, rugs, and cushions. These materials introduce essential warmth and comfort.

Natural Elements:
- Include subtle organic textures through elements like woven baskets, soft wood grains, and artisan ceramics, fostering visual warmth and emotional grounding.

Balanced Integration:
- Balance smooth textures (glass, polished wood) with tactile softness, creating subtle yet engaging visual contrast.

Zen-Inspired Decorative Elements

Decor in Zen-inspired Japandi living rooms must be meaningful, intentionally minimal, and visually calming:

Minimalist Art and Objects:
- Display carefully selected artwork, ceramics, or sculptural pieces sparingly, ensuring each object enhances tranquility and emotional resonance.

Botanical Simplicity:
- Integrate simple botanical elements—such as single-stem floral arrangements or minimal greenery—to subtly evoke nature and tranquility.

Soft Lighting:
- Choose warm, layered lighting with subtle fixtures, including Japanese-inspired paper lanterns, Scandinavian-style floor lamps, or gentle sconces, promoting relaxation and comfort.

Furniture Layout for Mindfulness and Connection

Furniture arrangement profoundly impacts Zen-inspired Japandi living rooms:

Open and Airy Layouts:
- Arrange furniture to maintain openness and visual clarity, carefully respecting negative space for tranquility and mental calmness.

Conversational Groupings:
- Position seating arrangements intuitively to encourage comfortable conversation and meaningful connections, reflecting hygge-inspired warmth and intimacy.

Balanced Symmetry and Asymmetry:
- Consider subtle asymmetrical arrangements or gentle symmetry for visual balance and emotional harmony, echoing Zen aesthetics.

Practical Tips for a Zen-inspired Japandi Living Room

To practically achieve Zen-inspired Japandi elegance, follow these guidelines:

Declutter Regularly:
- Keep your living room uncluttered and serene through regular, intentional editing of unnecessary items.

Mindful Selection:
- Carefully evaluate every item for genuine emotional and functional value, prioritizing objects that enhance tranquility and comfort.

Softness and Comfort Check:
- Regularly assess your room's comfort, ensuring seating, textiles, and decor remain physically comfortable and emotionally nurturing.

Creating a Zen-inspired Japandi living room requires thoughtful attention to furniture, color, texture, decor, and layout. By skillfully balancing minimalist clarity with tactile warmth and emotional serenity, your living room becomes a genuine sanctuary—a luxurious, comforting space dedicated to mindfulness, relaxation, and harmonious living.

Furniture Arrangement: The Art of Negative Space

In Japandi design, furniture arrangement is as much about what is left empty as what is included. Mastering negative space—often referred to in Japanese aesthetics as "Ma"—is fundamental to creating balanced, peaceful interiors. Negative space isn't emptiness; it's intentional breathing room that emphasizes visual clarity, promotes mindfulness, and highlights the beauty of each carefully selected piece. Arranging furniture thoughtfully to respect negative space is crucial in achieving true Japandi harmony, elevating interiors from merely elegant to profoundly serene.

Understanding Negative Space ("Ma")

In Japanese aesthetics, "Ma" is the carefully considered pause or empty interval between objects. This concept deeply influences Japandi design, where empty spaces are as valuable as filled ones. "Ma" fosters visual simplicity, emotional calmness, and intuitive flow throughout interiors, allowing each element to breathe and resonate fully. Properly utilized negative space has profound benefits:

- Visual Calmness: Creates interiors that feel tranquil, uncluttered, and relaxing.
- Enhanced Focus: Draws attention to essential furniture pieces, art, and decorative elements.
- Mindfulness and Harmony: Encourages mindful engagement with surroundings, fostering deeper appreciation and emotional serenity.

Practical Guidelines for Furniture Arrangement

Thoughtful furniture placement involves conscious decisions about both occupied and unoccupied spaces:

1. Prioritize Visual Breathing Room
   - Allow generous spacing between furniture items to maintain visual openness. Avoid overcrowding rooms or clustering items unnecessarily.
2. Create Intentional Focal Points
   - Highlight specific furniture or decorative elements by leaving purposeful empty space around them, enhancing their visual impact.
3. Establish Natural Flow and Circulation
   - Arrange furniture intuitively, allowing natural pathways for movement and comfortable interaction, ensuring rooms feel accessible and harmonious.

Arranging Furniture for Balanced Interiors

To achieve visual and emotional harmony through negative space, consider these arrangement strategies:

Minimalist Groupings
- Group furniture in minimal yet comfortable configurations—such as simple seating clusters, paired chairs, or carefully centered tables—to maintain clarity while fostering intimacy.

Balanced Symmetry or Subtle Asymmetry
- Choose symmetrical arrangements for formal tranquility or gentle asymmetry for a subtly dynamic yet serene effect. Balance empty space with carefully placed furniture for optimal visual harmony.

Scaled Proportions
- Carefully scale furniture relative to room size, ensuring neither too large nor too small. Proper scaling preserves negative space effectively, enhancing emotional tranquility and visual openness.

Negative Space in Different Living Areas

Furniture arrangement principles apply differently in each living space:

Living Rooms
- Arrange seating for comfortable conversation, leaving open areas around seating groups to ensure visual serenity and ease of movement.

Bedrooms
- Maintain openness around beds, keeping side tables or benches minimal and thoughtfully placed. Preserve spaciousness, promoting restful sleep and emotional peace.

Dining Rooms
- Center dining tables within rooms, leaving ample space around the table to move comfortably, enhancing both function and visual calmness.

Entryways and Hallways
- Keep these areas deliberately uncluttered, placing only essential pieces like benches or minimal storage to welcome guests with serene simplicity.

Common Mistakes to Avoid

Avoiding typical furniture arrangement mistakes is critical to preserving negative space effectively:

Overcrowding:
- Resist filling empty areas unnecessarily. Keep arrangements spacious to maintain Japandi's signature serenity.

Ignoring Scale:
- Furniture that's too large or small can disrupt negative space. Always carefully assess furniture size relative to room dimensions.

Excessive Symmetry:
- While symmetry offers balance, excessive symmetry can create visual rigidity. Introduce subtle asymmetry occasionally to maintain a gentle visual dynamic.

Practical Exercises: Mastering Negative Space

Develop your skill in balancing negative space practically:

Edit Your Rooms:
- Temporarily remove non-essential items. Gradually reintroduce only necessary furniture, observing how each piece affects negative space and visual harmony.

Visualize Space:
- Use masking tape or floor plans to visualize furniture placement before committing, assessing negative space visually and practically.

Observe Mindfully:
- Regularly evaluate your interiors, noting areas that feel cluttered or visually heavy. Adjust placement to restore openness and calmness.

By thoughtfully embracing the art of negative space in your Japandi furniture arrangements, your home achieves visual clarity, emotional tranquility, and timeless sophistication. Each carefully positioned piece contributes meaningfully to an overall atmosphere of serene luxury, reflecting the refined mindfulness at the heart of Japandi design.

Integrating Minimalist Comfort with Functionality

Japandi design elegantly bridges two seemingly opposite ideals: minimalist aesthetics and genuine comfort. The secret to this balance lies in skillfully integrating comfort with practical functionality. A truly harmonious Japandi interior is both visually minimalist and intuitively comfortable, reflecting an effortless blend of aesthetics and usability. Understanding how to thoughtfully merge these qualities will ensure your spaces feel inviting, serene, and seamlessly practical—embodying the very heart of Japandi luxury.

Understanding Minimalist Comfort

Minimalist comfort isn't about stark emptiness, nor is it about overly plush indulgence. Instead, it embodies a carefully curated balance—visual simplicity blended with inviting textures, ergonomic design, and thoughtful practicality. Japandi's minimalist comfort ensures every room feels calming and emotionally nurturing without compromising visual serenity.

Essential Elements of Minimalist Comfort:
Ergonomic Design:
- Furniture designed for natural comfort—gently curved chairs, supportive seating, and intuitively placed surfaces—ensures physical well-being.

Tactile Warmth:
- Subtle yet soft textures, such as linen, wool, cotton, and natural wood, introduce warmth and emotional comfort without visual clutter.

Intentional Simplicity:
- Every object and furnishing is thoughtfully chosen for clear purpose, emphasizing calmness and mindful living.

Combining Comfort and Functionality

Integrating comfort with functionality requires selecting furniture and design elements that embody practical elegance. Furniture and decor must serve real-life needs while preserving Japandi's signature minimalism:

Functional Furniture Choices:
Multi-purpose Designs:
- Opt for furniture offering dual functionality—such as benches with integrated storage, extendable dining tables, or convertible seating arrangements—maximizing practicality without cluttering spaces.

Built-in Storage Solutions:
- Incorporate subtle, built-in storage within furniture, cabinetry, or architectural features, keeping surfaces uncluttered while offering discreet yet essential practicality.

High-Quality Craftsmanship:
- Select furniture crafted from durable, quality materials designed to withstand daily use gracefully, maintaining elegance and usability long-term.

Practical Applications in Key Spaces

Effectively merging minimalist comfort and functionality varies by room:

Living Rooms
- Choose visually serene yet deeply comfortable sofas or lounge chairs.
- Incorporate functional coffee tables with hidden storage compartments or modular designs for flexible arrangements.

Bedrooms
- Select low-profile beds with integrated storage or minimalist bedside tables offering subtle practicality.
- Prioritize luxurious yet simple bedding and textiles, creating restful, visually tranquil spaces.

Kitchens and Dining Rooms
- Opt for streamlined cabinetry, practical storage solutions, and multifunctional kitchen islands.
- Select dining tables combining minimalist aesthetics with extendable or hidden functionalities for flexible usability.

Enhancing Comfort through Lighting and Texture

Lighting and texture significantly impact minimalist comfort and functionality:

Thoughtful Lighting:
- Prioritize layered lighting with soft ambient sources (pendant lamps, recessed lights), practical task lighting (desk lamps, under-cabinet lights), and comforting accents (floor lamps, candles), ensuring visual comfort and functional illumination.

Tactile Textures:
- Layer subtly textured textiles—soft rugs, linen curtains, knitted throws—balancing visual minimalism with sensory comfort.
- Use natural materials like smooth stone, warm wood, and artisan ceramics for enriching, comforting textures that enhance emotional warmth without visual clutter.

Intentional Placement for Comfort and Function

Furniture placement profoundly influences minimalist comfort and intuitive functionality:

Mindful Layouts:
- Arrange furniture intuitively, supporting natural movement, easy interaction, and visual clarity.

Balanced Proportions:
- Carefully scale furniture relative to room size, ensuring neither visual emptiness nor overcrowding disrupts comfort or practicality.

Strategic Comfort Zones:
- Create designated comfort zones within larger rooms—reading corners, conversation areas, meditation spaces—using furniture placement and soft textures to foster emotional nurturing and restful comfort.

Avoiding Common Pitfalls

Maintain minimalist comfort and functionality by avoiding common mistakes:

Over-Furnishing:
- Resist the temptation to overcrowd spaces with excessive furniture or decor. Always prioritize simplicity, practical use, and emotional comfort.

Sacrificing Practicality for Aesthetics:
- Never choose aesthetics over usability. Ensure furniture, layouts, and materials support genuine daily needs.

Neglecting Textural Warmth:
- Do not overlook textures and softness, which significantly impact emotional comfort. Balance minimalism with tactile warmth thoughtfully.

Practical Tips for Integrating Comfort and Functionality

Regular Evaluation:
- Frequently assess rooms for comfort and practicality. Adjust arrangements or replace pieces as necessary to maintain balanced harmony.

Mindful Selection:
- Before introducing new items, clearly evaluate their practicality and comfort, ensuring each addition enhances rather than diminishes Japandi harmony.

Continuous Refinement:
- Maintain visual clarity and comfort through continuous, intentional editing of your spaces, regularly removing unnecessary or uncomfortable items.

Integrating minimalist comfort with functionality is at the heart of Japandi luxury. By thoughtfully balancing these qualities—selecting ergonomic, multifunctional furniture, prioritizing warm textures and mindful placement—you transform your interiors into spaces that deeply resonate emotionally, visually, and practically. Your Japandi home thus becomes a sophisticated yet genuinely inviting sanctuary—beautifully minimal, intuitively comfortable, and perfectly functional for daily living.

CHAPTER 15
SERENE BEDROOMS & BATHROOMS

Minimalist Bedroom Retreats

A Japandi bedroom is more than just a place to sleep—it's a personal sanctuary designed for deep rest, emotional tranquility, and quiet rejuvenation. Creating a minimalist bedroom retreat involves thoughtful attention to furniture, colors, textures, and layout, seamlessly merging Japanese minimalism with Scandinavian comfort. The goal is an uncluttered yet cozy environment that encourages relaxation, mindfulness, and a restful atmosphere.

The Essence of a Japandi Bedroom

Japandi bedrooms embody simplicity, serenity, and comfort. They reflect a balance between minimalist aesthetics and welcoming warmth, carefully designed to soothe the senses and quiet the mind. By thoughtfully curating each element within your bedroom, you create a calming space that not only looks beautiful but fosters genuine emotional peace and restorative sleep. Key principles of Japandi bedroom design include:

- Minimalism: Reducing visual clutter to maintain tranquility.
- Comfort: Choosing luxurious yet simple bedding and textiles for sensory warmth.
- Nature Integration: Incorporating natural materials and subtle greenery to foster connection with the natural world.

Choosing Furniture with Purpose

Furniture in a Japandi bedroom must be carefully selected for both form and function:

Low-profile Beds:
- Inspired by Japanese tradition, low-profile beds foster grounding and visual serenity. Opt for simple wooden frames, ideally crafted from oak, ash, or bamboo, with minimal detailing to maintain a clean aesthetic.

Minimalist Side Tables:
- Choose simple, functional side tables with subtle storage or clean surfaces to hold essentials like books or lamps without adding clutter.

Integrated Storage Solutions:
- Consider built-in wardrobes or hidden storage under beds to keep rooms spacious and uncluttered, reinforcing emotional tranquility.

Calming Color Palettes for Restful Sleep

Color significantly impacts emotional calmness and restful sleep. Japandi bedrooms thrive with palettes that emphasize tranquility and harmony:

Warm Neutrals:
- Choose soft whites, gentle creams, warm greys, or muted taupes for walls and bedding, fostering calm and restful atmospheres.

Subtle Earth Tones:
- Introduce muted, nature-inspired colors like gentle greens, soft blues, or subtle browns, creating a harmonious, serene connection with nature.

Minimal Contrast:
- Maintain a harmonious palette by limiting strong contrasts, preserving visual tranquility essential for restful environments.

Textural Warmth: Softness in Simplicity

Textural richness enhances minimalist bedrooms, balancing visual simplicity with tactile comfort:

Natural Bedding:
- Choose bedding crafted from soft linen, crisp cotton, or gentle wool, ensuring tactile luxury and emotional comfort without visual clutter.

Tactile Accessories:
- Integrate cozy throws, plush rugs, or soft cushions sparingly to create warmth, carefully balancing tactile richness with visual minimalism.

Organic Textures:
- Complement textiles with natural materials such as wood, bamboo, or ceramics to subtly enrich the bedroom with emotional warmth.

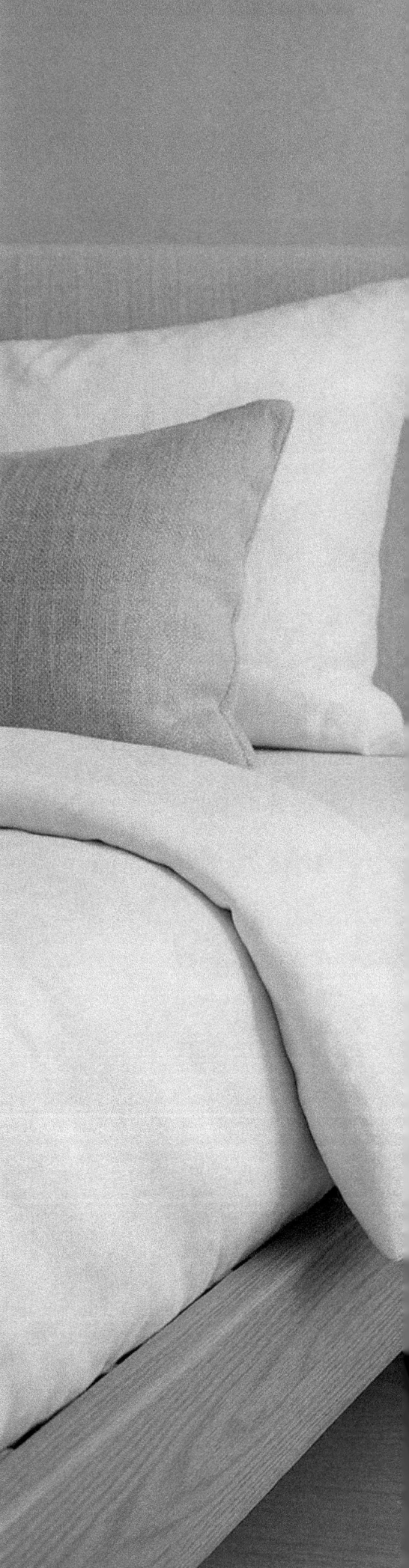

Zen-Inspired Decorative Touches

Decorative elements in Japandi bedrooms should be carefully curated, enhancing tranquility rather than cluttering it:

Minimalist Art:
- Choose simple, calming artwork or subtle abstract pieces that gently complement the space without overwhelming it.

Botanical Simplicity:
- Introduce a minimal amount of greenery or delicate floral arrangements, enhancing emotional calmness and a gentle connection to nature.

Soft Lighting:
- Prioritize warm, layered lighting—gentle bedside lamps, discreet wall sconces, or subtle recessed fixtures—creating soothing and restful illumination.

Layouts that Foster Relaxation and Calmness

Furniture layout profoundly influences bedroom tranquility:

Balanced Symmetry:
- Use symmetrical arrangements of bedside tables or lighting for formal tranquility, fostering visual harmony and emotional calmness.

Open Circulation Paths:
- Arrange furniture to allow intuitive, comfortable movement, creating peacefulness through visual openness and ease of use.

Mindful Positioning:
- Orient beds to maximize natural views or gentle daylight, enhancing relaxation and emotional serenity.

Practical Tips for Maintaining Your Minimalist Retreat

Maintaining your Japandi bedroom's tranquility requires ongoing mindfulness:

Routine Decluttering:
- Regularly edit your bedroom items, keeping only essential and emotionally meaningful objects.

Mindful Selection:
- Before adding new items, carefully evaluate their practical use, visual impact, and emotional resonance, ensuring harmony and tranquility.

Comfort Checks:
- Regularly reassess your bedroom for comfort—bedding softness, lighting warmth, furniture ergonomics—making adjustments to maintain restful comfort.

Creating a minimalist Japandi bedroom retreat is an intentional, rewarding process. By thoughtfully selecting furniture, embracing calming colors, balancing tactile warmth, and carefully curating decor and layout, you transform your bedroom into a sanctuary genuinely conducive to emotional peace, mindful living, and restful sleep. Your Japandi bedroom thus becomes a luxurious haven—simple, serene, and perfectly comforting.

Bedding and Textiles: Softness Meets Simplicity

In Japandi bedroom retreats, bedding and textiles play a crucial role—quietly shaping a room's emotional warmth, visual tranquility, and tactile luxury. These elements are essential for transforming minimalist bedrooms into genuinely comforting sanctuaries. By thoughtfully combining softness with simplicity, you create spaces that encourage restful sleep, emotional calmness, and sensory comfort—perfectly embodying Japandi's harmonious balance between minimalism and coziness.

The Importance of Softness and Simplicity

Japandi bedding and textiles blend tactile softness with understated elegance. The goal is to achieve genuine comfort without sacrificing visual minimalism. Each fabric choice—whether linen, cotton, wool, or silk—should reflect a mindful approach, enhancing emotional tranquility, tactile warmth, and aesthetic simplicity.

Essential Japandi Bedding: Quiet Luxury

Choosing the right bedding materials is critical for a restful Japandi retreat. Preferred fabrics combine practical luxury with subtle sophistication:

Linen Bedding
- Linen's naturally breathable, softly textured weave perfectly suits Japandi aesthetics.
- Its effortless drape and relaxed elegance foster tranquility, comfort, and luxurious simplicity.

Cotton Bedding
- Pure cotton sheets and duvet covers offer unmatched softness, everyday practicality, and visual simplicity.
- High-quality cotton provides gentle luxury while maintaining minimalist clarity.

Silk Accents
- Silk pillowcases or subtle silk accents introduce a refined, luxurious feel without overwhelming minimalist aesthetics.
- Their gentle sheen and soft texture enhance visual sophistication and emotional calmness.

Textiles for Emotional Warmth

Beyond bedding, textiles significantly influence a Japandi bedroom's emotional comfort and warmth:

Wool Throws and Blankets
- Wool introduces tactile warmth, comfort, and hygge-inspired coziness essential in colder climates.
- Choose neutral-colored wool throws or knitted blankets for subtle visual texture and emotional warmth.

Area Rugs
- Soft wool or cotton rugs provide visual anchoring, physical warmth, and tactile luxury, complementing minimalist flooring.
- Select rugs in gentle, muted colors to maintain visual harmony and tranquility.

Decorative Cushions
- Add sparingly placed decorative cushions crafted from linen, wool, or soft cotton to subtly enhance tactile comfort without cluttering simplicity.

Harmonious Color Choices for Textiles

Color is pivotal in ensuring Japandi textiles enhance emotional tranquility and aesthetic minimalism:

Neutral Foundations:
- Choose bedding and primary textiles in calm neutrals like soft whites, gentle creams, warm greys, or subtle taupes, fostering serene, restful atmospheres.

Muted Earthy Tones:
- Introduce accent textiles—throws, pillows, rugs—in muted earth tones such as sage green, dusty rose, gentle blues, or soft terracotta for subtle visual warmth.

Minimal Contrast:
- Maintain low contrast and harmonious combinations of colors to preserve emotional calmness and visual tranquility.

Balancing Softness with Minimalism

Integrating bedding and textiles effectively requires balancing tactile softness with visual minimalism:

Mindful Layering:
- Thoughtfully layer bedding, throws, and cushions, ensuring each addition enhances comfort without creating visual clutter.

Intentional Placement:
- Strategically position textiles—such as draping blankets naturally over beds or carefully arranging pillows—to subtly enhance comfort and visual elegance.

Textural Contrast:
- Complement smooth, minimalist furniture surfaces with gentle textile textures, creating subtle visual interest without overwhelming simplicity.

Caring for Your Japandi Textiles

Proper maintenance preserves the beauty and comfort of your Japandi bedding and textiles:

Routine Care:
- Regularly wash bedding and textiles gently according to fabric-specific guidelines, preserving texture and softness.

Protective Storage:
- Properly store seasonal textiles—such as wool blankets or spare bedding—in breathable storage bags, maintaining freshness and fabric integrity.

Quality Investment:
- Invest in high-quality, durable textiles that age gracefully and require minimal maintenance, embodying Japandi's mindful, long-term approach.

By thoughtfully selecting and integrating bedding and textiles in your Japandi bedroom, you achieve a luxurious yet serene environment perfectly aligned with Japandi principles. Softness and simplicity combine effortlessly, creating an atmosphere of restful calmness, genuine comfort, and sophisticated minimalism—transforming your bedroom into a true Japandi sanctuary.

Bathroom Design: Spa-like Elegance & Zen Calmness

Japandi bathrooms embody spa-like luxury combined with Zen serenity, transforming an everyday space into a deeply restorative retreat. The essential elements of Japandi bathroom design—clean lines, minimal clutter, natural materials, and tactile softness—create an atmosphere that promotes relaxation, mindfulness, and tranquility. A thoughtfully designed Japandi bathroom encourages calm routines, restful rituals, and emotional rejuvenation, elevating simple acts of self-care into luxurious, mindful experiences.

Creating a Spa-Like Atmosphere

To achieve spa-like elegance, focus on elements that elevate comfort, tranquility, and sensory indulgence without sacrificing Japandi minimalism:

Essential Spa-Like Features:
Freestanding Bathtubs:
- Deep, minimalist freestanding tubs provide visual elegance, relaxation, and restorative bathing experiences reminiscent of high-end spas.

Open, Airy Showers:
- Frameless glass showers or open wet-room layouts enhance visual openness, tranquility, and refined minimalism.

Heated Flooring:
- Underfloor heating introduces subtle luxury, comfort, and warmth, enhancing daily rituals.

Ambient Lighting:
- Subtle, layered lighting—such as recessed lights, minimalist sconces, and softly glowing pendants—fosters relaxation, calmness, and emotional comfort.

Zen-Inspired Minimalism and Clarity

Maintaining visual clarity and emotional serenity requires deliberate minimalism:

Clean Lines and Simple Fixtures:
- Choose sleek, minimalist faucets, sinks, and cabinetry that reflect elegant simplicity and effortless practicality.

Neutral and Muted Color Schemes:
- Employ soft whites, pale greys, earthy taupes, or subtle greens to enhance visual serenity and Zen-like tranquility.

Minimal Visual Clutter:
- Opt for hidden or discreet storage solutions, ensuring surfaces remain visually uncluttered and calming.

Natural Materials: Organic Luxury

Japandi bathrooms thrive with carefully chosen natural materials, enhancing visual authenticity, emotional warmth, and tactile luxury:

Stone Surfaces:
- Opt for subtle stone choices like honed marble, travertine, or limestone for countertops, flooring, or wall accents, providing quiet luxury and refined texture.

Warm Wood Accents:
- Introduce wood through vanity cabinetry, shelves, benches, or wall panels, adding warmth and organic authenticity.

Handcrafted Ceramics:
- Integrate artisanal ceramics for sinks, decorative bowls, or subtle decor accents, celebrating craftsmanship and emotional resonance.

Textural Softness and Comfort

Softness in Japandi bathrooms enhances emotional warmth and physical comfort without visual distraction:

Luxurious Towels:
- Choose plush cotton or linen towels in muted, neutral colors, subtly enhancing visual warmth and tactile comfort.

Minimalist Bath Mats:
- Include soft wool or cotton bath mats that complement the serene palette while adding functional softness.

Subtle Textile Accents:
- Sparingly integrate textile accessories such as linen curtains, woven baskets, or knitted storage, introducing subtle tactile richness.

Incorporating Nature and Greenery

Adding subtle elements of nature fosters tranquility and emotional calmness:

Minimalist Greenery:
- Integrate simple plant arrangements—small potted plants, bamboo stalks, or minimalist floral accents—to promote natural serenity.

Organic Decor:
- Display subtle natural elements—such as river stones, driftwood, or artisan ceramics inspired by nature—supporting Zen-like simplicity and emotional grounding.

Mindful Storage Solutions

Effective storage solutions enhance practicality without compromising visual simplicity:

Built-in Cabinetry:
- Employ integrated cabinets or drawers with clean, minimalist lines and discreet handles, maintaining visual calmness and functional storage.

Floating Shelves:
- Use simple, floating wooden shelves sparingly, providing practical storage and display without cluttering space.

Hidden Storage Compartments:
- Include subtle hidden compartments in vanity units or mirrors, ensuring toiletries and essentials remain easily accessible yet visually discreet.

Lighting for Zen Calmness

Carefully designed lighting profoundly influences Japandi bathroom serenity:
Warm, Layered Lighting:
- Combine ambient, task, and accent lighting strategically, ensuring bathrooms remain functional yet inviting and calm.

Natural Light:
- Maximize natural daylight through frosted windows or subtle blinds, providing gentle, diffused illumination that enhances tranquility.

Practical Tips for Japandi Bathroom Maintenance

Maintain your luxurious Zen-inspired bathroom with mindful care:

Regular Cleaning:
- Regularly clean surfaces gently with eco-friendly products, preserving the beauty and functionality of your bathroom.

Clutter Management:
- Routinely declutter, keeping only essential and emotionally meaningful items visible.

Comfort Checks:
- Periodically reassess your bathroom's comfort and functionality, making adjustments to maintain its restorative atmosphere.

By thoughtfully integrating spa-like elegance, Zen calmness, natural materials, and mindful minimalism, your Japandi bathroom becomes a deeply restorative retreat. Each carefully chosen element supports emotional tranquility, luxurious practicality, and serene aesthetics, transforming daily routines into genuinely comforting, mindful experiences.

Effective Japandi Storage Solutions

In Japandi interiors, effective storage solutions are essential. They allow you to maintain visual tranquility, eliminate clutter, and ensure spaces remain peaceful and serene. Japandi storage seamlessly integrates functionality with minimalist aesthetics, enhancing practicality without compromising visual harmony. By prioritizing simplicity, subtlety, and intuitive organization, you can achieve storage that feels effortlessly elegant, emotionally calming, and genuinely luxurious.

The Importance of Mindful Storage in Japandi

Mindful storage aligns closely with Japandi's minimalist philosophy. Effective storage solutions allow you to keep daily essentials organized and accessible, while maintaining clear, serene spaces. In Japandi bedrooms and bathrooms especially, thoughtful storage directly contributes to restful environments, emotional clarity, and visual tranquility.

Key qualities of Japandi storage include:

- Minimalist Design: Clean, streamlined shapes and subtle detailing.
- Hidden Functionality: Discreet compartments or concealed storage to maintain uncluttered surfaces.
- Natural Materials: Sustainably sourced wood, bamboo, or natural fibers ensuring visual warmth and emotional authenticity.

Essential Japandi Bedroom Storage

Bedrooms require effective storage that preserves calm and visual serenity:

Built-in Wardrobes
- Integrate custom-built wardrobes with minimalist facades and discreet hardware, seamlessly blending into wall spaces, maximizing storage without visual clutter.

Under-Bed Storage
- Choose low-profile beds with hidden drawers or lift-up mattress platforms, ensuring ample yet visually discreet storage.

Minimalist Bedside Storage
- Opt for simple side tables with small drawers or shelves, providing practical bedside storage while maintaining visual calmness.

Essential Japandi Bathroom Storage

Bathrooms benefit from subtle storage solutions that emphasize practicality and serenity:

Floating Vanities
- Install wall-mounted vanities featuring sleek, minimalist drawers or cabinets, providing accessible storage while maintaining visual openness and ease of cleaning.

Recessed Niches
- Incorporate built-in niches or recessed shelves within shower or bath areas, offering subtle, practical storage without disturbing visual tranquility.

Minimal Shelving
- Use minimalist floating shelves sparingly for towels, toiletries, or decorative items, ensuring essentials are accessible yet visually harmonious.

Storage Solutions for Living Areas

Living spaces require intuitive storage solutions that balance visual serenity and practicality:

Multifunctional Furniture
- Invest in benches, ottomans, or coffee tables with integrated storage compartments, ensuring practicality without compromising minimalism.

Sleek Sideboards
- Choose sideboards with clean lines, discreet sliding doors, or hidden compartments, offering generous storage while enhancing visual simplicity.

Modular Shelving Systems
- Incorporate wall-mounted, modular shelving units with customizable configurations, allowing flexible storage solutions that evolve with your needs.

Essential Features of Japandi Storage Design

To ensure effective Japandi storage, focus on these essential design elements:

Clean Lines and Simplicity:
- Select furniture and cabinetry with sleek, minimalist forms, subtle detailing, and seamless surfaces to maintain calm, uncluttered spaces.

Natural Materials and Finishes:
- Prioritize sustainably sourced wood, bamboo, or matte natural finishes, reinforcing visual warmth and emotional authenticity.

Discreet Hardware:
- Choose cabinetry with minimalist or integrated hardware, ensuring functionality without visual distraction.

Concealed Storage Compartments:
- Opt for furniture and cabinetry featuring hidden drawers, discreet compartments, or sliding doors, maintaining minimalist elegance and intuitive practicality.

Practical Tips for Maximizing Japandi Storage Efficiency

Maximize Japandi storage efficiency through mindful planning and regular organization:

Routine Decluttering:
- Regularly evaluate belongings, removing unnecessary items and ensuring storage spaces remain functional, organized, and serene.

Mindful Organization:
- Organize essentials intuitively within storage spaces, keeping frequently used items easily accessible and neatly arranged.

Custom Solutions:
- Consider custom-built storage to precisely match your specific spatial dimensions and organizational needs, ensuring optimal use of available space.

CHAPTER 16
THE JAPANDI KITCHEN & DINING

Designing Calm, Functional Kitchens

A Japandi kitchen masterfully blends calm aesthetics with intuitive functionality. In this space, the art of simplicity meets everyday practicality, creating an environment that feels peaceful, inviting, and effortlessly functional. To design a truly serene and practical Japandi kitchen, you must focus on clean lines, purposeful layouts, sustainable materials, and minimalist storage solutions. The result is a kitchen that not only looks beautiful but also supports mindful cooking, relaxed dining, and genuine comfort.

The Essence of a Japandi Kitchen

Japandi kitchens represent the harmonious balance between visual serenity and functional efficiency. They emphasize minimal clutter, streamlined organization, and carefully curated aesthetics, ensuring the kitchen remains a welcoming and calming hub of your home. The goal is a kitchen that encourages mindfulness in meal preparation, simplicity in daily routines, and emotional tranquility at all times.

Key Principles for Japandi Kitchens

To effectively design a Japandi kitchen, focus on these essential principles:

1. Visual Simplicity and Clarity
   - Keep surfaces and layouts clean and uncluttered, promoting visual calmness and easy maintenance.
   - Select cabinetry with minimal hardware, sleek facades, and subtle finishes, enhancing aesthetic simplicity.
2. Functional Elegance
   - Prioritize ergonomic layouts, intuitive storage, and practical fixtures, ensuring daily kitchen tasks remain effortless and enjoyable.
   - Invest in high-quality appliances with minimalist designs and quiet operations, reinforcing a calm kitchen atmosphere.
3. Natural Materials and Sustainability
   - Choose sustainable materials—solid wood cabinetry, bamboo accents, stone countertops—that enhance authenticity and visual warmth.
   - Integrate eco-friendly and responsibly sourced materials, aligning your kitchen's luxury with mindful environmental responsibility.

Creating a Calm, Harmonious Layout

The kitchen layout profoundly influences the room's serenity and functionality:

Open and Airy Design:
- Opt for open-plan kitchens with generous negative space, creating visual openness, emotional calmness, and ease of movement.

Intuitive Work Triangle:
- Arrange appliances, sinks, and preparation areas in an efficient work triangle, maximizing functionality while maintaining minimalist simplicity.

Dedicated Zones:
- Designate clear functional zones for cooking, preparation, storage, and dining, supporting intuitive usability and visual harmony.

Cabinetry and Storage: Subtle Practicality

Storage solutions in Japandi kitchens emphasize subtlety and discreet practicality:

Minimalist Cabinetry:
- Install cabinetry with clean lines, minimal detailing, and hidden handles, maintaining visual calmness and unobtrusive practicality.

Integrated Appliances:
- Integrate appliances—fridges, dishwashers, ovens—behind cabinetry fronts or within seamless layouts, enhancing visual harmony.

Efficient Organization:
- Incorporate interior organization systems such as pull-out drawers, hidden compartments, and custom shelving to ensure everyday essentials remain organized and easily accessible.

Harmonious Materials and Textures

Material choices profoundly impact the kitchen's aesthetic serenity and emotional comfort:

Natural Wood:
- Choose sustainably sourced wood or bamboo cabinetry, countertops, or shelving to add visual warmth, tactile luxury, and emotional authenticity.

Stone and Quartz:
- Incorporate elegant, subtly veined stone countertops—marble, quartz, or limestone—that offer durable practicality and understated luxury.

Subtle Ceramic and Glass:
- Include artisanal ceramic tiles or simple glass backsplash elements, enriching textural contrast without disrupting minimalist aesthetics.

Calm, Inviting Lighting

Lighting significantly influences kitchen serenity:

Soft Ambient Lighting:
- Utilize warm, ambient ceiling lighting to create a calming overall atmosphere, enhancing comfort during meal preparation and dining.

Practical Task Lighting:
- Install discreet under-cabinet or pendant lighting for focused illumination on cooking and prep areas, maintaining functionality without visual distraction.

Natural Daylight:
- Maximize natural daylight through minimalist window treatments or skylights, reinforcing emotional tranquility and visual openness.

Zen-Inspired Decor and Accessories

Decorative elements should remain minimal yet meaningful, complementing the kitchen's serenity:

Subtle Botanicals:
- Incorporate simple plant arrangements or minimal floral accents, introducing natural warmth without cluttering spaces.

Artisan Accents:
- Display carefully selected ceramics, wooden objects, or simple artworks sparingly, enhancing emotional resonance and refined simplicity.

Minimalist Functional Accessories:
- Choose elegantly minimalist accessories—ceramic vessels, wooden cutting boards, subtle textiles—that reinforce both practical usability and visual harmony.

Practical Tips for Japandi Kitchen Maintenance

Regular maintenance ensures your Japandi kitchen remains calm, functional, and aesthetically pristine:

Routine Cleaning:
- Maintain cleanliness through regular, gentle cleaning of surfaces and cabinetry, preserving visual elegance and practical functionality.

Mindful Decluttering:
- Routinely reassess kitchen items, removing unnecessary objects to maintain visual clarity and emotional tranquility.

Periodic Organization:
- Regularly reorganize drawers and cabinets to ensure intuitive accessibility, functional efficiency, and visual harmony.

Dining in Japandi: Warmth and Simplicity at the Table

Dining in a Japandi-inspired space is a deeply intentional experience, thoughtfully blending warmth, simplicity, and refined minimalism. It's about creating an environment where every meal becomes a serene moment—an intimate gathering that nurtures connection, comfort, and mindfulness. By carefully selecting furniture, tableware, lighting, and decor, your Japandi dining area becomes an inviting space, beautifully balanced between Scandinavian coziness and Japanese clarity.

The Essence of Japandi Dining

The Japandi dining space harmonizes two distinct yet complementary philosophies:

Japanese Simplicity:
- Emphasizes visual clarity, clean lines, and mindful minimalism, fostering emotional calmness and tranquility.

Scandinavian Warmth:
- Prioritizes comfort, practicality, and inviting softness, creating intimate atmospheres ideal for connecting with loved ones over shared meals.

By effectively merging these elements, your dining space will support daily rituals of mindful eating and comforting socialization, reinforcing emotional warmth and visual serenity.

Selecting the Perfect Dining Furniture

Japandi dining furniture must balance minimalism, comfort, and elegance:

Dining Tables:
Simple, Clean-lined Designs:
- Choose dining tables with minimalist profiles, clean edges, and refined detailing, crafted from solid wood—such as oak or ash—for timeless warmth and visual clarity.

Functional Elegance:
- Opt for extendable or modular dining tables for flexible seating arrangements and everyday practicality.

Dining Chairs:
Comfortable Minimalism:
- Select chairs with ergonomic forms and soft curves, upholstered in neutral-toned natural fabrics or featuring subtle, refined woodcraft.

Timeless Design:
- Classic Scandinavian designs, such as wishbone chairs, or Japanese-inspired minimalist seating, reinforce visual harmony and tactile comfort.

Creating a Harmonious Color Palette

Color choices significantly impact the emotional warmth and visual tranquility of your dining space:

Neutral Foundations:
- Use muted tones such as gentle whites, soft creams, warm greys, or earthy taupes for walls, furniture, and textiles, creating calm, inviting backdrops.

Subtle Contrasts:
- Introduce restrained contrasts—such as pale sage green accents, muted terracotta elements, or gentle blues—through tableware, decor, or subtle textiles to enrich visual warmth and emotional depth.

Textural Warmth and Softness

Japandi dining areas rely heavily on tactile warmth to balance visual minimalism:

Comforting Textiles:
- Include soft cushions, subtle table linens, or woven placemats, enhancing sensory warmth without cluttering simplicity.

Natural Wood:
- Prioritize dining tables and chairs crafted from smooth, gently textured wood, subtly reinforcing visual comfort and emotional warmth.

Organic Accents:
- Integrate artisanal ceramics, wooden bowls, or woven baskets sparingly for additional tactile depth and visual warmth.

Mindful Tableware and Decor Choices

Carefully curated tableware and decor significantly enhance your Japandi dining experience:

Minimalist Ceramics:
- Choose handcrafted ceramic plates, bowls, and serving vessels featuring subtle glazes and gentle irregularities, reflecting mindful luxury and authentic craftsmanship.

Simple Glassware:
- Select elegant, clear glassware with minimalist shapes, maintaining visual serenity while enhancing the refined dining experience.

Natural Elements:
- Introduce subtle botanical arrangements, small plants, or simple floral accents on tables or sideboards, fostering emotional tranquility and connection to nature.

Lighting for Warm, Inviting Dining

Lighting is crucial for maintaining Japandi's emotional warmth and visual comfort during meals:

Soft Ambient Lighting:
- Choose minimalist pendant lights or soft ceiling fixtures that cast gentle, warm illumination, creating welcoming atmospheres.

Intimate Accent Lighting:
- Incorporate candles or discreet table lamps to provide cozy, inviting warmth for evening dining and socializing.

Natural Daylight:
- Maximize natural daylight through sheer window treatments or minimalist blinds, fostering emotional tranquility and visual openness during daytime dining.

Layouts for Comfort and Connection

A thoughtful layout enhances dining comfort, social interaction, and emotional warmth:

Comfortable Seating Arrangements:
- Arrange chairs with adequate spacing for easy conversation, comfortable movement, and effortless usability.

Open and Uncluttered Flow:
- Maintain ample circulation space around tables and seating, reinforcing visual serenity and intuitive practicality.

Intimate Groupings:
- For larger spaces, create intimate seating areas or additional cozy spots—such as corner seating or minimalist benches—for enhanced emotional warmth and flexible usability.

Layouts for Comfort and Connection

A thoughtful layout enhances dining comfort, social interaction, and emotional warmth:

Comfortable Seating Arrangements:
- Arrange chairs with adequate spacing for easy conversation, comfortable movement, and effortless usability.

Open and Uncluttered Flow:
- Maintain ample circulation space around tables and seating, reinforcing visual serenity and intuitive practicality.

Intimate Groupings:
- For larger spaces, create intimate seating areas or additional cozy spots—such as corner seating or minimalist benches—for enhanced emotional warmth and flexible usability.

Practical Tips for Japandi Dining Spaces

Maintain your Japandi dining area's inviting simplicity through practical, regular maintenance:

Regular Decluttering:
- Routinely clear unnecessary items from dining tables and sideboards, maintaining visual calmness and emotional tranquility.

Mindful Setting:
- Set tables intentionally and simply, using minimal yet elegant tableware, textiles, and decor, enhancing mindful dining experiences.

Routine Comfort Checks:
- Regularly assess seating comfort, lighting warmth, and overall functionality, adjusting as needed to preserve emotional comfort and visual elegance.

By thoughtfully integrating warmth, simplicity, intentional furniture selections, mindful decor, and comforting textures, your Japandi dining space becomes a genuinely inviting retreat. Each carefully curated element enriches daily dining rituals, promoting mindfulness, connection, and emotional serenity—creating spaces that perfectly reflect Japandi's refined simplicity and comforting luxury.

Selecting Timeless Tableware and Ceramics

In Japandi dining spaces, tableware and ceramics transcend mere practicality. They embody mindful elegance, subtle craftsmanship, and timeless appeal, turning every meal into a serene ritual. Carefully chosen ceramics and tableware profoundly influence the dining experience, enhancing emotional comfort, visual harmony, and tactile luxury. To authentically embrace Japandi dining, prioritize handcrafted pieces, minimalist aesthetics, subtle imperfections, and refined simplicity, creating a table setting that invites tranquility, mindfulness, and genuine beauty.

The Essence of Japandi Tableware

Japandi tableware combines Japanese minimalism with Scandinavian warmth, creating pieces that feel genuinely timeless and quietly luxurious. The goal is to choose items that enhance daily rituals, resonate emotionally, and foster serene dining experiences. Timeless tableware elevates every meal, encouraging mindfulness and appreciation through thoughtfully designed forms, subtle textures, and authentic craftsmanship.

Choosing the Perfect Ceramics

Ceramics are the heart of Japandi tableware, prized for their handmade authenticity, tactile comfort, and visual subtlety:

Artisan Craftsmanship
- Select ceramics handcrafted by skilled artisans, featuring gentle irregularities, unique glazes, and subtle imperfections, celebrating the Japanese philosophy of Wabi-Sabi—beauty found in imperfection.

Minimalist Shapes
- Choose ceramics with clean, simple shapes—shallow bowls, elegant plates, minimalist cups—that effortlessly blend visual serenity with functional practicality.

Neutral and Muted Colors
- Opt for ceramics in muted, neutral tones such as soft whites, gentle greys, earthy taupes, or subtle pastel shades, harmonizing beautifully with Japandi's calming aesthetics.

Essential Japandi Tableware Pieces

Selecting key tableware items thoughtfully ensures your Japandi dining experience feels harmonious, luxurious, and timeless:

Dinnerware
- Invest in high-quality, minimalist dinnerware sets featuring plates, bowls, and serving dishes crafted from artisanal ceramics or porcelain. Subtle designs and matte glazes enhance visual elegance and tactile comfort.

Drinkware
- Choose simple yet refined glassware or ceramic cups. Opt for clear, minimalist drinking glasses, handcrafted ceramic mugs, or traditional Japanese-inspired tea cups, ensuring visual simplicity and emotional comfort.

Serving Pieces
- Include minimalist serving platters, bowls, and trays crafted from ceramics, sustainably sourced wood, or subtle stoneware. These pieces provide functional elegance and refined beauty during gatherings or everyday meals.

Selecting Timeless Flatware and Accessories

Complement your ceramics with carefully selected flatware and accessories that reinforce Japandi's timeless aesthetics:

Flatware
- Choose flatware with clean lines, minimalist designs, and subtle finishes—matte stainless steel, muted gold, or brushed silver. Avoid excessive ornamentation, ensuring visual calmness and enduring appeal.

Table Linens
- Use natural, sustainable textiles—such as linen placemats, cotton napkins, or gentle wool table runners—in muted, neutral colors to subtly enrich texture and emotional warmth.

Minimalist Decorative Objects
- Integrate sparingly placed decorative elements—such as handcrafted wooden spoons, ceramic salt cellars, or small botanical arrangements—enhancing visual interest and tactile comfort without cluttering simplicity.

Harmonious Integration and Display

Mindful integration and thoughtful display elevate the Japandi dining aesthetic:

Minimalist Arrangements:
- Arrange tableware carefully, leaving ample space around each piece to enhance visual tranquility and emotional calmness.

Open Shelving:
- Display your ceramics, glassware, and accessories on minimalist open shelves or subtle cabinetry, celebrating craftsmanship and beauty without visual clutter.

Intentional Settings:
- Set tables simply, using carefully chosen tableware, flatware, and textiles to create harmonious, elegant presentations that enrich dining experiences.

Caring for Your Timeless Japandi Tableware

Preserving the beauty and functionality of your ceramics and tableware requires gentle, mindful care:

Regular Maintenance:
- Wash ceramics gently by hand using mild, eco-friendly soaps. Avoid harsh chemicals or abrasive tools that can damage delicate glazes or finishes.

Careful Storage:
- Store ceramics and tableware thoughtfully—stack gently, separate delicate items, and maintain clean, dry storage conditions to prevent damage.

Mindful Handling:
- Handle ceramics and delicate tableware carefully during use and washing, preserving their subtle craftsmanship and timeless beauty.

By carefully selecting and thoughtfully integrating timeless tableware and ceramics, your Japandi dining space becomes a sophisticated yet serene environment that enriches everyday experiences. Each handcrafted piece enhances emotional tranquility, refined simplicity, and enduring luxury, turning every meal into a meaningful ritual of mindful elegance and genuine beauty.

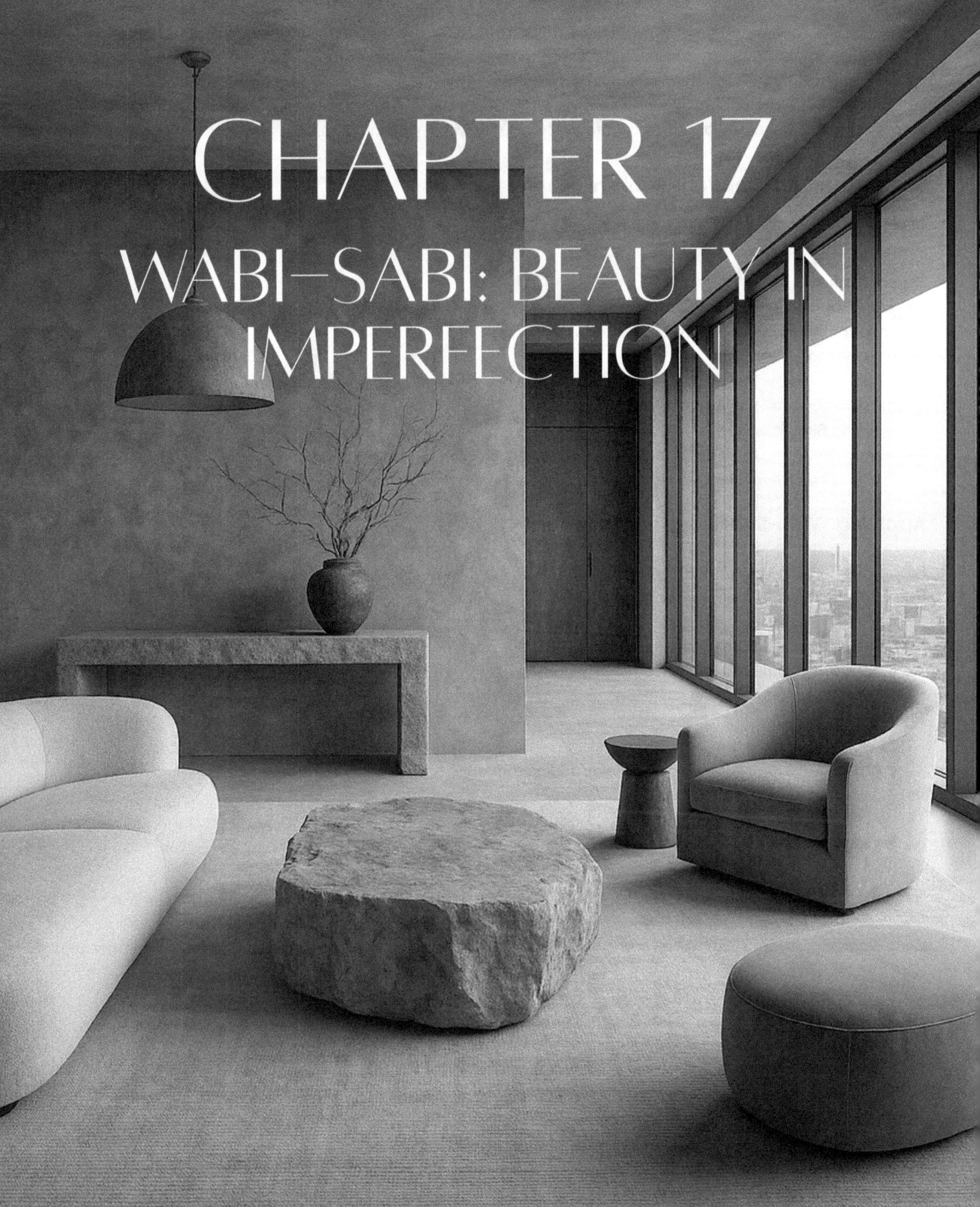

CHAPTER 17
WABI-SABI: BEAUTY IN IMPERFECTION

Embracing Imperfection: Philosophy and Practice

At the heart of Japandi design lies Wabi-Sabi—an ancient Japanese philosophy that celebrates beauty in imperfection, impermanence, and incompleteness. Wabi-Sabi embraces authenticity, simplicity, and humility, encouraging us to appreciate the subtle charm of natural wear, handmade irregularities, and objects touched by time. Integrating Wabi-Sabi into your home isn't merely about aesthetics; it's a mindful practice that fosters emotional depth, genuine warmth, and profound tranquility within your interiors.

Understanding the Wabi-Sabi Philosophy

To truly embrace Wabi-Sabi, it's essential to understand its core concepts:

Imperfection
- Wabi-Sabi recognizes beauty in natural flaws—cracks, uneven textures, and subtle irregularities. These imperfections represent authenticity and individuality.

Impermanence
- It appreciates the transient, ever-changing nature of life. Materials and objects gracefully aging—patina, fading, gentle wear—are valued rather than hidden.

Humility and Simplicity
- It emphasizes modesty and simplicity, encouraging intentional, humble living and mindful consumption. Spaces are curated with meaningful, simple objects, fostering emotional serenity.

Applying Wabi-Sabi in Japandi Interiors

Practical application of Wabi-Sabi philosophy involves carefully curating and intentionally arranging objects and furniture to highlight authenticity and imperfection:

Choosing Natural, Authentic Materials
- Embrace materials like raw or reclaimed wood, handcrafted ceramics, aged stone, or softly worn textiles. These materials beautifully age over time, enhancing emotional depth and visual warmth.

Appreciating Handmade Craftsmanship
- Select furniture and decor crafted by artisans, intentionally embracing gentle irregularities, visible craftsmanship, and subtle imperfections, adding authenticity and emotional resonance.

Allowing Natural Aging and Patina
- Value furniture or objects that gently age—such as leather developing a soft patina, metals tarnishing slightly, or wood surfaces subtly weathering—acknowledging beauty in impermanence.

Wabi-Sabi and Minimalism: Harmonious Balance

Wabi-Sabi and Japandi minimalism complement each other beautifully, balancing visual simplicity with emotional depth:

Intentional Placement:
- Carefully place furniture and decor with mindful consideration, emphasizing each item's beauty and uniqueness through spacious, uncluttered surroundings.

Selective Imperfection:
- Include only select items embodying authentic imperfections, ensuring they stand out beautifully without overwhelming minimalist serenity.

Quiet Elegance:
- Curate spaces thoughtfully, focusing on quiet, subtle elegance rather than overt luxury. Choose fewer, deeply meaningful pieces over numerous superficial items.

Cultivating a Mindful Wabi-Sabi Mindset

Fully embracing Wabi-Sabi involves shifting your mindset towards greater mindfulness and emotional depth:

Mindful Selection:
- Choose furniture and decor intentionally, focusing on emotional resonance, authentic beauty, and genuine craftsmanship over superficial perfection.

Acceptance of Imperfection:
- Develop an emotional appreciation for natural imperfections, subtle irregularities, and gentle wear, fostering a deeper connection with your surroundings.

Simplicity and Contentment:
- Prioritize simplicity and mindfulness in your daily life, appreciating fewer but meaningful possessions, nurturing emotional contentment and tranquility.

Common Misconceptions and How to Avoid Them

To authentically embrace Wabi-Sabi, avoid common misconceptions:

Wabi-Sabi ≠ Shabby or Neglected:
- Genuine Wabi-Sabi objects aren't carelessly damaged or overly worn. They reflect gentle, intentional aging or authentic, skilled craftsmanship rather than neglect.

Balance Imperfection:
- Maintain a harmonious balance between imperfection and refined minimalism, ensuring interiors remain emotionally soothing and visually elegant rather than chaotic or cluttered.

Emotional Authenticity:
- Choose Wabi-Sabi elements genuinely resonating emotionally rather than solely following trends, preserving meaningful connections and authentic interiors.

Practical Exercises to Embrace Wabi-Sabi

Integrate Wabi-Sabi philosophy practically into your home and lifestyle through these mindful exercises:

Curate Your Space:
- Periodically reassess your interiors, mindfully curating items that genuinely embody Wabi-Sabi—authentic imperfections, subtle aging, emotional resonance.

Mindful Observance:
- Regularly observe your surroundings, consciously appreciating subtle imperfections, craftsmanship, and gentle wear in daily life, cultivating deeper emotional appreciation.

Mindful Acquisition:
- When acquiring new items, intentionally select pieces reflecting genuine authenticity, natural materials, skilled craftsmanship, and emotional warmth, embracing Wabi-Sabi thoughtfully.

Incorporating Handmade Objects & Artisanal Details

In Japandi interiors, handmade objects and artisanal details hold profound significance. They celebrate human creativity, skilled craftsmanship, and authentic beauty, enhancing interiors with emotional warmth and subtle elegance. Carefully selected handcrafted pieces imbue your home with genuine uniqueness and mindful luxury, adding depth, character, and soul to your minimalist spaces. Incorporating artisanal objects effectively supports both visual tranquility and emotional resonance, harmonizing perfectly with the Japandi and Wabi-Sabi philosophies.

Why Handmade Objects Matter in Japandi

Handmade objects resonate deeply because they embody authenticity, thoughtful craftsmanship, and intentional imperfection. Each artisanal piece is unique, carrying the emotional imprint of the maker, enriching your interiors beyond purely aesthetic considerations. They foster deeper connections, emotional warmth, and mindful appreciation—qualities essential to genuine Japandi spaces.

Key benefits of handmade and artisanal objects include:

- Emotional Resonance: Authentic handmade pieces carry meaningful stories, enhancing emotional connection and warmth.
- Visual and Tactile Beauty: Skilled craftsmanship introduces subtle textures, gentle irregularities, and refined detailing, enriching visual elegance and tactile comfort.
- Sustainability and Ethical Luxury: Supporting artisans and handmade objects promotes responsible, mindful consumption, aligning with Japandi's ethical values.

Essential Artisanal Elements for Japandi Interiors

Selecting appropriate artisanal pieces thoughtfully enhances your Japandi spaces:

Ceramics and Pottery
- Choose handcrafted ceramics—vases, bowls, cups, or tableware—featuring gentle imperfections, unique glazing, and minimalist shapes, adding subtle elegance and emotional authenticity.

Textiles
- Integrate artisanal textiles such as handwoven wool rugs, linen throws, or cotton cushions, each piece showcasing craftsmanship, natural textures, and emotional warmth.

Wooden Furniture and Decor
- Select handcrafted wooden furniture—tables, chairs, shelving—or subtle decor items (bowls, trays), highlighting visible joinery, skilled detailing, and natural, sustainably sourced wood.

Integrating Handmade Objects Thoughtfully

Effective integration of handmade pieces ensures harmony and enhances emotional resonance:

Intentional Placement
- Arrange handmade objects sparingly and intentionally, allowing each piece to stand out beautifully without visual clutter. Provide generous negative space around items, enhancing visual and emotional appreciation.

Complementary Harmony
- Choose artisanal objects that harmonize visually with your interiors—select items crafted in muted, neutral colors, natural materials, and subtle textures that complement Japandi's minimalist serenity.

Balanced Imperfection
- Balance handcrafted imperfection with refined simplicity. Combine handmade elements thoughtfully with clean-lined furniture and subtle textures, ensuring interiors remain elegant and emotionally calming.

Supporting Artisans and Ethical Craftsmanship

Selecting artisanal objects involves mindful, ethical considerations:

Transparent Sourcing:
- Choose objects from artisans or brands that transparently share information about their materials, sourcing, and production processes.

Local and Independent Makers:
- Prioritize purchasing from local artisans or small-scale makers, supporting ethical craftsmanship and regional economic sustainability.

Sustainable Practices:
- Ensure handmade objects are produced sustainably, with responsibly sourced materials, eco-friendly processes, and minimal environmental impact.

Caring for Your Handmade Objects

Thoughtful care preserves the beauty and longevity of artisanal pieces:

Gentle Cleaning:
- Regularly clean handcrafted objects carefully with mild, natural cleaning solutions. Avoid harsh chemicals or abrasive materials that can damage delicate finishes.

Mindful Storage:
- Store delicate handmade textiles, ceramics, or decor thoughtfully—wrapped carefully or stored neatly—to maintain their integrity and beauty.

Routine Appreciation:
- Regularly reassess handmade objects, rearranging occasionally to renew emotional appreciation and visual harmony within your spaces.

Practical Exercises for Incorporating Handmade Objects

Cultivate a mindful approach to integrating handmade pieces through practical exercises:

Curate Mindfully:
- Regularly evaluate your interiors, carefully curating handmade objects to ensure emotional resonance, visual harmony, and mindful simplicity.

Engage with Craftsmanship:
- Learn about the artisans behind your handmade objects, deepening emotional connection and appreciation through understanding craftsmanship and production stories.

Selective Acquisition:
- Intentionally acquire new handmade objects thoughtfully—choose items based on genuine emotional resonance, authenticity, and enduring beauty rather than impulsive purchases.

By intentionally incorporating handmade objects and artisanal details into your Japandi spaces, you create interiors that deeply resonate emotionally, visually, and ethically.

CHAPTER 18
JAPANDI AND NATURE

Biophilic Design: Bringing the Outdoors In

At the heart of Japandi design lies a profound connection to nature, beautifully embodied in the principles of biophilic design. Biophilic design is an approach that integrates natural elements into interior spaces, fostering emotional tranquility, enhancing well-being, and strengthening our innate bond with nature. In Japandi interiors, biophilic design goes beyond mere aesthetics—it deeply enriches living environments, transforming homes into serene sanctuaries of natural warmth, organic beauty, and mindful harmony.

Understanding Biophilic Design

Biophilic design centers on humanity's inherent need for nature. It integrates natural elements into living spaces, creating calming, restorative environments that enhance emotional well-being, productivity, and overall quality of life. Key aspects of biophilic design include:

Visual Connection to Nature:
- Incorporating natural views, indoor plants, and organic materials to create a visual connection with the natural world.

Natural Light:
- Maximizing exposure to daylight, improving mood, circadian rhythms, and overall health.

Organic Materials and Textures:
- Utilizing materials like wood, stone, ceramics, and textiles, promoting tactile comfort and emotional warmth.

Integrating Biophilic Elements in Japandi Interiors

To effectively bring the outdoors into your Japandi home, focus on these practical biophilic strategies:

Enhancing Natural Light
Open Layouts and Large Windows:
- Design interiors with spacious layouts and expansive windows to flood spaces with natural daylight, creating visual openness and emotional comfort.

Translucent or Minimal Window Treatments:
- Use sheer curtains, minimalist blinds, or shoji-inspired screens to gently filter daylight, maintaining privacy while enhancing tranquility.

Incorporating Greenery and Plants
Strategically Placed Indoor Plants:
- Introduce carefully selected plants—such as fiddle-leaf figs, snake plants, or bonsai trees—in strategic locations, providing visual freshness, emotional serenity, and subtle natural beauty.

Minimalist Botanical Displays:
- Employ minimalist botanical arrangements or simple floral accents, maintaining visual clarity while subtly enriching interiors with organic warmth.

Using Organic and Natural Materials
Sustainable Wood and Bamboo:
- Incorporate sustainably sourced wood or bamboo for flooring, furniture, or architectural features, enhancing natural authenticity and tactile luxury.

Stone and Earthy Ceramics:
- Utilize natural stone surfaces or handcrafted ceramics in subtle earth tones, providing emotional grounding, visual warmth, and tactile comfort.

Benefits of Biophilic Design in Japandi Spaces

Integrating biophilic elements within Japandi interiors offers profound emotional, physical, and aesthetic benefits:

Enhanced Emotional Well-being:
- Connection with nature promotes calmness, reduces stress, and improves mood, creating emotionally soothing interiors.

Improved Physical Health:
- Natural lighting and air-purifying plants improve air quality, regulate circadian rhythms, and enhance overall health.

Visual Serenity and Aesthetic Balance:
- Organic elements and natural textures enrich visual aesthetics, fostering interiors that feel naturally balanced, harmonious, and visually pleasing.

Benefits of Biophilic Design in Japandi Spaces

Integrating biophilic elements within Japandi interiors offers profound emotional, physical, and aesthetic benefits:

Enhanced Emotional Well-being:
- Connection with nature promotes calmness, reduces stress, and improves mood, creating emotionally soothing interiors.

Improved Physical Health:
- Natural lighting and air-purifying plants improve air quality, regulate circadian rhythms, and enhance overall health.

Visual Serenity and Aesthetic Balance:
- Organic elements and natural textures enrich visual aesthetics, fostering interiors that feel naturally balanced, harmonious, and visually pleasing.

Practical Application in Different Rooms

Biophilic design principles apply uniquely within each living space:

Living and Dining Areas
- Embrace large windows, indoor plants, and natural materials, creating inviting social spaces deeply connected to nature.

Bedrooms
- Introduce subtle greenery, natural textiles, and abundant daylight, fostering restful environments that promote emotional tranquility and restorative sleep.

Bathrooms
- Integrate natural stone, plants, and wood accents, transforming bathrooms into spa-like retreats filled with soothing organic elements.

Home Offices
- Utilize natural light, greenery, and organic materials to create productive, calming spaces, enhancing focus and emotional comfort during work.

Maintaining Biophilic Balance

Ensuring your Japandi home remains harmonious and balanced involves mindful biophilic integration:

Balance Nature and Minimalism:
- Thoughtfully balance natural elements with minimalist aesthetics—avoid overcrowding spaces with excessive greenery or organic decor. Choose fewer, meaningful biophilic elements that enhance visual and emotional serenity.

Mindful Selection:
- Select natural materials, plants, and decor intentionally, prioritizing emotional resonance, authenticity, and enduring beauty over superficial trends or clutter.

Regular Maintenance:
- Regularly care for indoor plants and natural materials—routine watering, pruning, cleaning—to ensure lasting beauty, health, and visual harmony.

Practical Exercises for Embracing Biophilic Design

Develop a deeper biophilic connection through these mindful exercises:

Mindful Plant Selection:
- Intentionally select plants for specific spaces, considering their emotional impact, visual beauty, and practical maintenance.

Nature Observation:
- Regularly spend mindful moments appreciating natural elements within your home—plants, daylight patterns, organic textures—cultivating deeper emotional connection and appreciation.

Curated Natural Elements:
- Periodically assess and curate natural elements in your spaces, ensuring each item genuinely enriches your emotional tranquility and visual harmony.

By thoughtfully embracing biophilic design within your Japandi interiors, you create deeply restorative, emotionally soothing spaces filled with natural beauty, organic warmth, and profound tranquility. Each biophilic element—whether natural lighting, subtle greenery, or authentic materials—strengthens your emotional connection to nature, transforming your home into a serene sanctuary of mindful luxury and timeless elegance.

Plants and Organic Elements

Integrating plants and organic elements into Japandi interiors is essential for creating spaces that truly resonate emotionally and visually. Plants, natural textures, and organic materials infuse your home with life, freshness, and tactile warmth, beautifully complementing Japandi's serene minimalism. Thoughtfully chosen and intentionally placed greenery and natural decor elevate your interiors, providing emotional comfort, visual harmony, and a profound connection to the natural world.

The Importance of Plants in Japandi Design

Plants are integral to Japandi interiors, bringing multiple benefits:

Emotional Tranquility:
- Plants foster emotional calmness, reduce stress, and create soothing atmospheres, enhancing well-being and mindfulness.

Visual Freshness:
- Greenery introduces vibrant, fresh aesthetics that complement the minimalist palette, adding subtle yet impactful visual interest.

Air Quality and Health:
- Indoor plants improve air quality by naturally purifying the air, supporting better physical health and well-being.

Selecting the Perfect Plants for Japandi Interiors

Ideal plants for Japandi design balance visual simplicity with natural elegance, requiring minimal maintenance:

Fiddle-Leaf Fig (Ficus lyrata)
- Provides dramatic yet minimalist impact with large, sculptural leaves.
- Ideal as a striking focal point in living areas or bedrooms.

Snake Plant (Sansevieria trifasciata)
- Offers architectural simplicity, air purification, and easy maintenance.
- Perfect for minimalistic spaces or subtle accent locations.

Bonsai and Miniature Trees
- Beautifully embody Japanese aesthetics, offering emotional tranquility and refined natural beauty.
- Ideal for tables, shelves, or minimalist displays.

Peace Lily (Spathiphyllum)
- Features graceful, simple white blooms and lush greenery.
- Excellent for subtly adding emotional calmness and visual softness.

Incorporating Plants Mindfully

Effectively integrating plants into your Japandi interiors requires thoughtful placement and mindful selection:

Minimalist Groupings:
- Use plants sparingly, placing individual plants or small groups intentionally, enhancing visual calmness and avoiding clutter.

Strategic Placement:
- Position plants to enhance interiors visually and emotionally—use larger plants as focal points or subtle greenery to soften minimalist spaces.

Natural Containers:
- Choose simple, elegant planters crafted from ceramic, wood, or stone, reinforcing visual harmony and natural authenticity.

Organic Elements: Natural Beauty and Texture

Beyond plants, other organic elements significantly enhance Japandi interiors:

Wood and Bamboo
- Use sustainably sourced wood or bamboo furniture, flooring, or decor elements, enriching interiors with warmth, authenticity, and tactile comfort.

Stone and Clay
- Integrate natural stone surfaces—such as marble or limestone countertops, floors, or decorative objects—and artisanal clay ceramics, providing emotional grounding, visual warmth, and subtle elegance.

Natural Textiles
- Incorporate organic textiles—linen, cotton, wool—within curtains, upholstery, or decor accents, enhancing tactile comfort, emotional warmth, and visual softness.

Harmonious Integration and Balance

Achieving visual harmony and emotional tranquility through plants and organic elements involves careful consideration:

Balance and Proportion:
- Maintain visual balance by carefully selecting plant sizes relative to your interiors, ensuring neither overwhelming nor overly sparse appearances.

Mindful Textural Contrast:
- Intentionally pair smooth surfaces—polished wood, glass—with subtly textured elements like woven baskets, soft textiles, or raw ceramics, creating balanced visual interest and emotional comfort.

Selective Simplicity:
- Curate interiors thoughtfully, choosing fewer meaningful organic elements, prioritizing authentic beauty and emotional resonance over excess or visual clutter.

Caring for Your Japandi Plants and Organic Elements

Effective care maintains your plants and natural decor's beauty, health, and visual harmony:

Routine Plant Care:
- Regularly water, prune, and dust indoor plants, ensuring optimal health, vibrant freshness, and emotional tranquility.

Mindful Cleaning:
- Gently clean organic materials—wood, ceramics, stone—with mild, eco-friendly solutions, preserving their natural beauty, texture, and authenticity.

Routine Reassessment:
- Periodically reevaluate your plants and organic decor, rearranging occasionally to refresh emotional appreciation and visual harmony within your interiors.

Practical Exercises for Integrating Plants and Organic Elements

Deepen your biophilic connections practically through mindful exercises:

Curate Intentionally:
- Regularly reassess and curate your plant arrangements and organic decor, ensuring visual harmony, emotional resonance, and mindful simplicity.

Mindful Plant Selection:
- Intentionally choose plants based on emotional impact, visual beauty, and practical care requirements, ensuring lasting satisfaction and well-being.

Nature Observation:
- Regularly engage in mindful observation of plants and organic materials within your home, cultivating deeper appreciation, emotional tranquility, and authentic connection to nature.

Lighting Choices: Natural and Subtle Illumination

Lighting in Japandi interiors is more than merely functional—it is a crucial design element deeply influencing mood, comfort, and visual tranquility. In Japandi spaces, lighting combines abundant natural daylight with soft, subtle artificial illumination, enhancing emotional warmth, visual clarity, and restful serenity. Thoughtfully selected and strategically placed lighting creates soothing, inviting interiors that beautifully reflect Japandi's harmonious balance of Japanese minimalism and Scandinavian coziness.

The Importance of Natural Lighting

Natural daylight is the cornerstone of Japandi lighting design, profoundly impacting physical and emotional well-being:

Enhanced Well-being:
- Natural light improves mood, reduces stress, and regulates circadian rhythms, fostering emotional tranquility and improved health.

Visual Openness and Serenity:
- Daylight visually expands interiors, creating a sense of spaciousness, clarity, and harmony.

Authentic Aesthetic Appeal:
- Natural lighting highlights organic textures, subtle colors, and minimalist details, enhancing visual elegance and authentic beauty.

Maximizing Natural Light

Effectively harness natural daylight through these practical strategies:

Expansive Windows and Open Layouts
- Incorporate large, minimalist windows and open-plan spaces, maximizing natural daylight and enhancing visual serenity.

Minimalist Window Treatments
- Opt for sheer curtains, translucent blinds, or Japanese-inspired shoji screens, gently diffusing daylight while preserving privacy and emotional tranquility.

Reflective Surfaces
- Employ subtle reflective surfaces—softly polished wood floors, mirrors, pale walls—to distribute natural light evenly, maintaining visual harmony and emotional comfort.

Subtle Artificial Illumination

Complement natural daylight with soft, subtle artificial lighting to maintain visual clarity, emotional warmth, and practical usability during evenings or low-light periods:

Ambient Lighting
- Use gentle ceiling fixtures, subtle pendant lights, or minimalist recessed lighting to softly illuminate rooms, creating comforting, inviting atmospheres.

Task Lighting
- Provide discreet yet effective task lighting—under-cabinet lighting, adjustable lamps, desk lights—ensuring practical functionality without visual distraction.

Accent Lighting
- Introduce warm accent lighting—soft wall sconces, table lamps, or candles—to enhance emotional intimacy, visual warmth, and comforting ambiance.

Ideal Japandi Lighting Fixtures

Select fixtures that beautifully align with Japandi's minimalist aesthetics and comforting warmth:

Paper Lanterns
- Embrace traditional Japanese-inspired paper lanterns or modern variations, providing soft, diffused illumination and gentle visual beauty.

Minimalist Pendants
- Choose sleek, minimalist pendant lamps crafted from natural materials—wood, bamboo, ceramic—creating visually elegant, softly illuminated interiors.

Subtle Wall Sconces
- Opt for subtle, minimalist wall sconces providing gentle, indirect lighting, enhancing visual tranquility and emotional comfort.

Strategic Lighting Placement

Thoughtful lighting placement profoundly influences Japandi interiors' serenity and usability:

Balanced Illumination:
- Distribute lighting evenly across spaces, avoiding overly bright or dark areas, maintaining visual harmony and emotional calmness.

Intuitive Functionality:
- Place task lighting intuitively in practical areas—kitchen countertops, reading corners, desks—ensuring effortless functionality and practical usability.

Emotional Ambiance:
- Position ambient and accent lighting to create warm, inviting atmospheres in social areas or restful corners, supporting emotional tranquility and comforting intimacy.

Harmonizing Lighting with Japandi Interiors

Achieve harmonious lighting through mindful consideration of aesthetics and practicality:

Color Temperature:
- Use warm-toned, soft white bulbs (2700-3000K) for artificial lighting, reinforcing Japandi's emotional warmth and visual softness.

Material and Texture Integration:
- Choose lighting fixtures crafted from natural materials or subtle textures—paper, ceramic, wood—harmonizing beautifully with Japandi's organic elements.

Minimal Visual Clutter:
- Select minimalist fixtures and discreet designs, maintaining visual simplicity and ensuring lighting enhances rather than distracts from interiors.

Caring for Your Japandi Lighting

Ensure long-lasting beauty and functionality through mindful lighting care:

Regular Maintenance:
- Periodically clean lighting fixtures gently to preserve their visual elegance, texture, and material integrity.

Bulb Selection:
- Consistently use appropriate bulbs—warm-toned LEDs—for visual and emotional comfort, energy efficiency, and lasting satisfaction.

Routine Adjustments:
- Regularly reassess lighting placements and effectiveness, adjusting as necessary to maintain optimal visual harmony, emotional tranquility, and practical usability.

Practical Exercises for Mindful Lighting Choices

Cultivate mindful lighting awareness through practical exercises:

Mindful Observation:
- Regularly observe lighting conditions in your interiors—daylight patterns, evening illumination—adjusting fixtures or treatments to enhance emotional tranquility and visual harmony.

Intentional Selection:
- Thoughtfully select new lighting fixtures based on aesthetics, emotional impact, and practical usability, prioritizing timeless designs and authentic materials.

Lighting Experimentation:
- Experiment periodically with different lighting arrangements—varying placement, fixtures, or bulb warmth—to refresh emotional appreciation and visual clarity within your spaces.

By thoughtfully integrating natural daylight and subtle artificial illumination, your Japandi interiors become inviting, serene spaces filled with visual clarity, emotional warmth, and profound comfort. Each carefully chosen lighting element enhances the aesthetic elegance, practical usability, and emotional tranquility of your home, perfectly capturing Japandi's mindful simplicity and timeless sophistication.

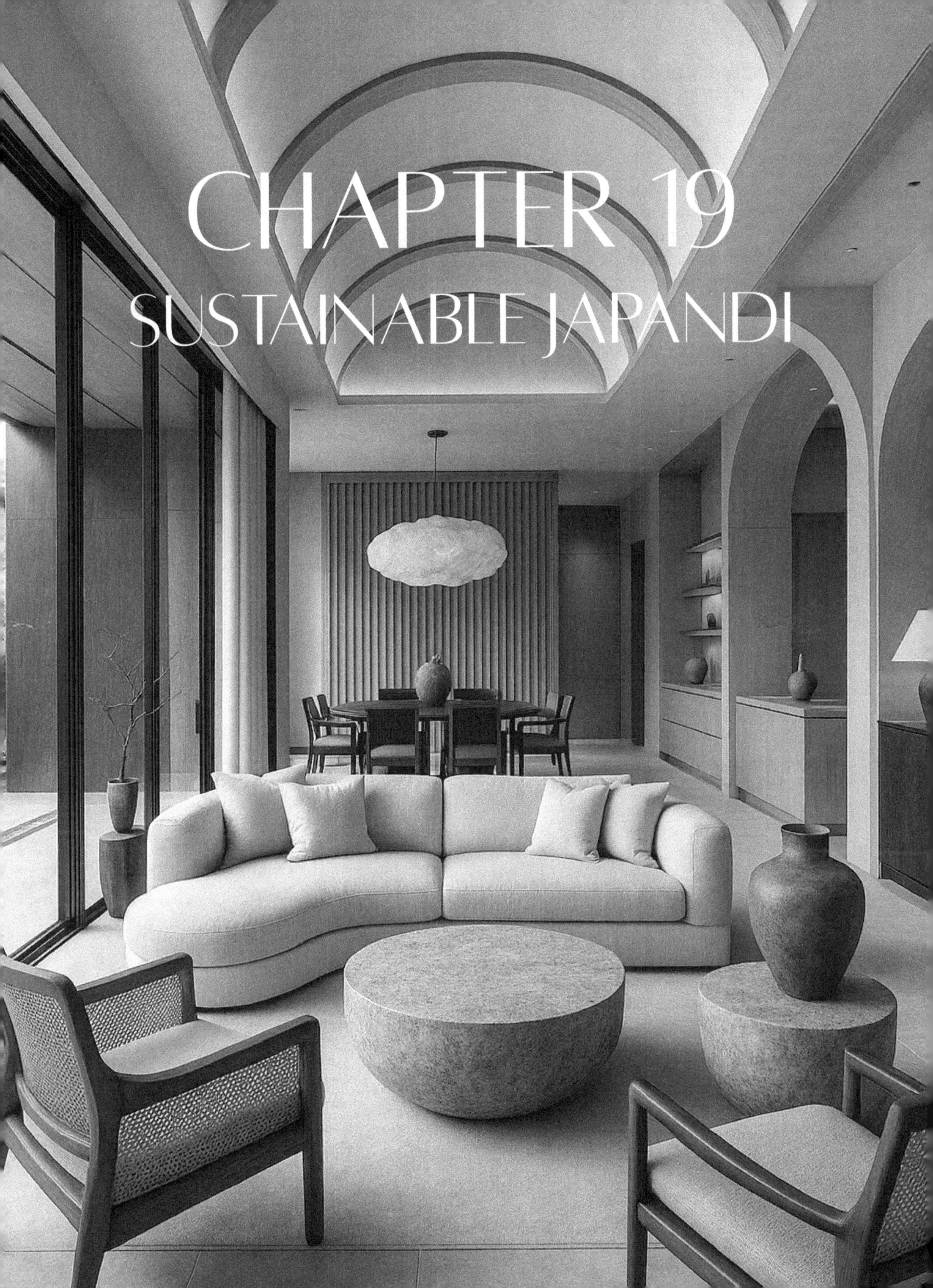

CHAPTER 19
SUSTAINABLE JAPANDI

Eco-friendly Interiors: Principles & Practices

Sustainability lies at the heart of authentic Japandi design. Eco-friendly Japandi interiors are thoughtfully designed, prioritizing environmental responsibility, mindful living, and ethical choices. Embracing sustainability in your home is more than a trend; it's a commitment to conscious living, long-term durability, and ethical luxury. By integrating sustainable principles and practices, your Japandi spaces become serene, responsible sanctuaries that deeply respect nature and reflect your values of mindfulness, simplicity, and environmental care.

Core Principles of Eco-friendly Japandi Design

To create genuinely sustainable interiors, Japandi design adheres to clear foundational principles:

1. Conscious Minimalism
   - Prioritize fewer, carefully chosen items that are meaningful, durable, and multifunctional, reducing waste and promoting mindful living.
2. Sustainable Materials
   - Use eco-friendly, responsibly sourced materials—such as FSC-certified wood, bamboo, natural textiles, or reclaimed elements—enhancing visual warmth and ethical authenticity.
3. Ethical Craftsmanship
   - Select furniture and decor from artisans or manufacturers committed to ethical labor practices, fair wages, and sustainable production methods.
4. Longevity and Durability
   - Choose high-quality items designed to withstand daily use gracefully, minimizing frequent replacements and supporting long-term sustainability.

Practical Strategies for Eco-friendly Japandi Interiors

Applying eco-friendly principles practically ensures your interiors remain beautifully sustainable:

Mindful Material Selection
- Choose natural, renewable, and responsibly harvested materials—solid wood, bamboo, cork, linen, organic cotton—ensuring minimal environmental impact.

Reducing Environmental Footprint
- Opt for energy-efficient lighting, natural insulation, and eco-friendly finishes or paints to minimize environmental harm and improve indoor air quality.

Recycling and Reclaimed Elements
- Incorporate reclaimed wood, vintage furniture, or repurposed materials into your interiors, significantly reducing waste and adding emotional authenticity.

Sustainable Japandi Furniture Choices

Furniture plays a critical role in sustainable Japandi interiors:

High-Quality Craftsmanship
- Invest in expertly crafted furniture designed for longevity—solid wood tables, durable sofas, ergonomic chairs—minimizing environmental impact through lasting durability.

Eco-friendly Materials
- Choose furniture constructed from sustainably sourced wood, bamboo, or recycled materials, aligning aesthetics, practicality, and sustainability.

Ethical Production
- Select furniture produced ethically, with transparent sourcing, fair labor practices, and minimal waste, supporting mindful consumption and ethical luxury.

Textiles and Soft Furnishings

Selecting eco-friendly textiles significantly enhances sustainable interiors:

Organic and Natural Fabrics:
- Prioritize textiles made from organic cotton, linen, hemp, or sustainably sourced wool, ensuring tactile comfort and environmental responsibility.

Durability and Quality:
- Invest in high-quality, durable textiles that age gracefully, maintaining beauty and minimizing frequent replacements.

Ethical Textile Production:
- Support producers committed to ethical labor practices, minimal environmental impact, and transparent sourcing of fibers and materials.

Mindful Decor and Accessories

Sustainable Japandi decor involves thoughtful selection of accessories:

Artisanal and Handmade Decor:
- Choose decor pieces handcrafted by local artisans, reducing transportation emissions, supporting local economies, and enriching interiors with authentic beauty.

Minimalism in Decor:
- Curate fewer, meaningful decorative items, preventing unnecessary consumption and visual clutter, promoting mindfulness and tranquility.

Upcycled or Vintage Elements:
- Integrate vintage or upcycled decor thoughtfully, enhancing emotional authenticity, reducing waste, and supporting sustainable living.

Eco-friendly Practices in Daily Life

Practical daily habits enhance your interior's sustainability:

Energy Efficiency:
- Adopt energy-saving habits—LED lighting, energy-efficient appliances, mindful consumption—to minimize environmental impact and enhance eco-friendly living.

Regular Maintenance:
- Maintain furniture, textiles, and decor carefully, extending their lifespan, preserving beauty, and reducing the need for replacements.

Mindful Consumption:
- Regularly evaluate purchases, prioritizing necessity, quality, and genuine emotional value, supporting long-term sustainability and minimal environmental impact.

Practical Exercises for Sustainable Japandi Living

Deepen your sustainability practices through mindful exercises:

Regular Interior Audits:
- Periodically assess your interiors, identifying opportunities to incorporate eco-friendly materials, sustainable furniture, or mindful decor.

Mindful Acquisition:
- Adopt intentional purchasing habits, thoroughly researching items before acquisition, prioritizing sustainability, ethical production, and long-term value.

Lifestyle Mindfulness:
- Incorporate sustainability practices into daily routines, consciously reducing waste, choosing eco-friendly products, and embracing mindful minimalism.

By thoughtfully integrating eco-friendly principles and sustainable practices, your Japandi interiors become elegant, responsible environments beautifully aligned with your values. Each carefully selected sustainable item, ethical practice, and mindful choice enriches your home, transforming your interiors into spaces deeply connected to nature, mindful living, and lasting tranquility—perfectly capturing Japandi's timeless simplicity and sustainable luxury.

Ethical Choices: Materials and Craftsmanship

At the core of sustainable Japandi design lies the thoughtful selection of ethical materials and responsible craftsmanship. These choices go beyond aesthetics—they reflect a commitment to mindfulness, sustainability, and fair labor practices. Incorporating ethical materials and artisanal craftsmanship into your Japandi interiors elevates your spaces with authenticity, emotional warmth, and environmental integrity, creating beautiful, conscious interiors aligned with your values.

Why Ethical Choices Matter in Japandi Design

Ethical choices in materials and craftsmanship deeply enrich Japandi interiors through meaningful connections, emotional resonance, and sustainable living:

Environmental Responsibility:
- Using responsibly sourced materials and eco-friendly practices minimizes environmental harm, ensuring sustainable luxury.

Fair Labor and Economic Impact:
- Supporting ethical craftsmanship promotes fair wages, safe working conditions, and positive economic impacts in local communities.

Mindful Living:
- Ethical choices foster mindfulness, intentional consumption, and deeper appreciation for quality, durability, and authenticity.

Selecting Ethical Materials

Thoughtfully choosing ethical materials is foundational to sustainable Japandi interiors:

Responsibly Sourced Wood
- Prioritize FSC-certified or locally harvested wood, ensuring sustainable forestry practices, biodiversity preservation, and minimal environmental impact.

Bamboo
- Opt for bamboo, a rapidly renewable resource offering durability, aesthetic elegance, and environmental responsibility.

Natural Textiles
- Choose organic and sustainably harvested textiles—linen, cotton, wool, hemp—for upholstery, bedding, and decor, ensuring comfort and ethical authenticity.

Recycled and Upcycled Materials
- Integrate furniture and decor crafted from recycled or reclaimed materials, significantly reducing waste and environmental footprint.

Embracing Ethical Craftsmanship

Ethical craftsmanship involves supporting skilled artisans and responsible production practices:

Fair Labor Practices
- Purchase furniture and decor from manufacturers committed to fair labor practices—ensuring safe working conditions, fair wages, and transparent sourcing.

Transparent Supply Chains
- Choose brands or artisans with transparent production processes and openly shared information about materials sourcing, manufacturing practices, and environmental impact.

Local and Independent Artisans
- Support local artisans and independent makers, reducing transportation emissions, sustaining local economies, and promoting authentic craftsmanship.

Embracing Ethical Craftsmanship

Ethical craftsmanship involves supporting skilled artisans and responsible production practices:

Fair Labor Practices
- Purchase furniture and decor from manufacturers committed to fair labor practices—ensuring safe working conditions, fair wages, and transparent sourcing.

Transparent Supply Chains
- Choose brands or artisans with transparent production processes and openly shared information about materials sourcing, manufacturing practices, and environmental impact.

Local and Independent Artisans
- Support local artisans and independent makers, reducing transportation emissions, sustaining local economies, and promoting authentic craftsmanship.

Ethical Choices in Furniture and Decor

Carefully select furniture and decor reflecting ethical practices:

Furniture
- Choose pieces crafted from ethically sourced materials, produced by manufacturers transparent about sourcing and committed to sustainability.

Textiles and Upholstery
- Select upholstery fabrics and textiles produced under fair labor conditions, using sustainable processes and organic materials.

Decorative Objects
- Integrate decor items handcrafted ethically by artisans, prioritizing authenticity, skilled craftsmanship, and emotional resonance.

Identifying Ethical Brands and Makers

Ensure authenticity by identifying truly ethical brands and artisans:

Certifications and Standards:
- Look for credible certifications such as FSC, Fair Trade, OEKO-TEX, or GOTS, ensuring verified sustainability and ethical practices.

Research Transparency:
- Thoroughly research brands' websites and materials, prioritizing those openly sharing sourcing details, manufacturing practices, and environmental commitments.

Community Reputation:
- Choose brands and artisans highly regarded for ethical standards, craftsmanship quality, and sustainability commitments within their communities.

Practical Tips for Ethical Japandi Living

Maintain ethical standards practically within daily life:

Mindful Purchases:
- Regularly evaluate new acquisitions, prioritizing ethical, sustainable, and high-quality choices that resonate emotionally and support mindful living.

Care and Maintenance:
- Thoughtfully maintain ethical furniture, textiles, and decor, extending their lifespan, preserving their beauty, and minimizing environmental impact.

Community Engagement:
- Support local artisans and ethical businesses, actively promoting sustainable economic practices and authentic craftsmanship within your community.

Practical Exercises for Ethical Choices

Deepen your commitment to ethical living through practical exercises:

Regular Interior Reviews:
- Periodically review your interiors, intentionally identifying opportunities to integrate ethical materials, support responsible craftsmanship, and enhance emotional authenticity.

Ethical Education:
- Continually educate yourself about sustainable materials, ethical production practices, and responsible brands, strengthening mindful decision-making and conscious living.

Intentional Acquisition:
- Practice mindful acquisition—carefully researching each item's ethical standards, production history, and environmental impact, ensuring lasting satisfaction and alignment with your values.

Longevity in Design: Choosing Quality over Quantity

Longevity is a foundational principle of Japandi design. Prioritizing quality over quantity ensures your home remains timeless, emotionally fulfilling, and environmentally responsible. Choosing pieces built for durability and enduring beauty aligns with Japandi's mindful approach, emphasizing thoughtful consumption and long-term sustainability. Longevity in design transforms your interiors into meaningful, tranquil spaces defined by lasting satisfaction, authentic craftsmanship, and refined simplicity.

Why Longevity Matters in Japandi Interiors

Embracing longevity means selecting fewer but higher-quality items designed to age gracefully, withstand daily use, and retain emotional resonance over time. The benefits are clear:

Environmental Sustainability:
- Reducing frequent replacements and waste through durable choices supports eco-friendly living.

Economic Mindfulness:
- Investing in fewer high-quality items proves economically wise, offering lasting value and timeless satisfaction.

Emotional Connection:
- Durable, high-quality items become meaningful possessions, deepening emotional connections and appreciation within your spaces.

Principles for Choosing Long-lasting Items

Effectively prioritizing longevity involves clear guiding principles:

1. Superior Craftsmanship
   - Select furniture and decor expertly crafted from robust materials—solid wood, durable metals, high-quality textiles—ensuring structural integrity, visual elegance, and lasting beauty.
2. Timeless Aesthetic
   - Choose pieces featuring minimalist, timeless designs rather than trend-driven elements, ensuring visual harmony, enduring appeal, and continued relevance.
3. Sustainable Materials
   - Prioritize sustainably sourced, responsibly produced materials designed for durability, eco-friendliness, and graceful aging.
4. Multifunctionality and Practicality
   - Opt for furniture and decor offering practical versatility, adaptability, and intuitive usability, promoting enduring satisfaction and purposeful living.

Selecting Long-lasting Japandi Furniture

Furniture significantly influences Japandi longevity:

Solid Wood Furniture:
- Choose furniture crafted from sustainably harvested hardwood—oak, walnut, ash—known for strength, durability, and elegant aging.

Ergonomic Comfort:
- Invest in ergonomically designed seating, beds, or tables crafted for both aesthetic simplicity and functional longevity, supporting lasting comfort and satisfaction.

Robust Construction:
- Prioritize furniture built using traditional, skilled joinery methods—such as dovetail or mortise-and-tenon—enhancing structural durability, authenticity, and refined aesthetics.

Long-lasting Textiles and Soft Furnishings

Choose textiles thoughtfully to enhance longevity:

High-Quality Fabrics:
- Select durable, natural textiles—linen, organic cotton, wool—resistant to wear and tear, maintaining beauty and tactile luxury over time.

Mindful Care:
- Properly maintain textiles through regular, gentle cleaning and careful storage, significantly extending their lifespan and preserving their appearance.

Neutral and Timeless Colors:
- Opt for timeless, neutral-colored textiles, ensuring enduring visual appeal, versatility, and emotional resonance across changing design preferences.

Decor and Accessories: Quality over Quantity

Effective Japandi longevity extends to decorative items:

Authentic Craftsmanship:
- Select decor objects handcrafted by skilled artisans, ensuring durable construction, emotional authenticity, and timeless elegance.

Minimalist Selection:
- Curate fewer meaningful decorative pieces, prioritizing quality craftsmanship and genuine emotional resonance rather than accumulating numerous lower-quality items.

Vintage and Antique Elements:
- Incorporate carefully chosen vintage or antique decor, inherently designed for longevity, emotional depth, and timeless appeal.

Practical Strategies for Long-lasting Interiors

Ensure your interiors remain beautiful, functional, and emotionally fulfilling long-term:

Regular Maintenance:
- Consistently maintain and care for furniture, textiles, and decor, preserving structural integrity, aesthetic beauty, and emotional satisfaction.

Mindful Replacement:
- Replace items thoughtfully, opting for high-quality, durable replacements aligned with Japandi aesthetics, sustainable materials, and enduring satisfaction.

Continuous Evaluation:
- Regularly evaluate your spaces, ensuring each piece retains practical usability, aesthetic harmony, and emotional resonance, adjusting thoughtfully as needed.

Practical Exercises for Longevity and Quality

Strengthen your commitment to longevity practically:

Quality Audits:
- Periodically audit your interiors, identifying and replacing low-quality items with thoughtfully chosen, durable pieces.
- Mindful Acquisition:
- Approach new purchases intentionally, carefully researching durability, craftsmanship, and aesthetic timelessness before investing.
- Lifestyle Mindfulness:
- Cultivate lifestyle practices prioritizing quality, durability, and intentional minimalism, continuously aligning your interiors with Japandi's sustainable, mindful philosophy.

BECOME ICONIC—MAKE YOUR STYLE VIRAL WITH US

You've selected "Less & Serene", a statement addition to your beautiful home.

Now it's your moment in the spotlight! Create a captivating video or sophisticated photograph featuring "Less & Serene" and share your creation on Instagram, TikTok, or Facebook using the hashtag #StudioLux. Your elegant post might just spark the next big social media trend!

Why participate?

- Showcase your exquisite taste and inspire a wide audience.
- Gain the opportunity to be featured by StudioLux for greater visibility and recognition.

And there's more to come...

CLAIM YOUR EXCLUSIVE GIFTS!

To celebrate your creativity, we've designed an exclusive bonus filled with practical and inspiring ideas you can immediately use to enhance your home's style. Don't miss this special opportunity—it's your next step toward achieving interior excellence.

Follow these simple steps to claim your reward:

1. Capture your unique photo or create a compelling video featuring the book.
2. Share your creation on Instagram, TikTok, or Facebook using the hashtag #StudioLux.
3. Scan the QR code below to instantly unlock your exclusive bonus content.

Your moment of viral fame awaits!
With style and appreciation,

StudioLux